THEN AND NOW

An Anderson Valley Journey

Featuring old and new photographs
of selected buildings and homes,
accompanied by brief histories.

WES SMOOT & STEPHEN SPARKS

CONTENTS

About the Authors vi

Acknowledgements viii

Introduction x

The View from Burger Rock and The Discovery of Anderson Valley xii

Map of Anderson Valley xvi

HIGHWAY 128

1.	48.50	L	Mountain House	2
2.	47.19	R	The Chatham Ranch—private driveway	4
3.	45.99	R	The Gaskill School House	6
4.	44.75	L	Morrow House	8
5.	44.01	R	Ingram House / Hill Ranch	10
6.	38.50	R	Yorkville Post Offices / 2nd P.O. / Ornbaun House	12
7.	38.33	R	Yorkville Hotel / McDonald's-to-the-Sea Highway	14

HIGHWAY 253 (Right off Highway 128 at sign to Ukiah)

8.	600 feet	R	Renus Burger Place / Johnson Ranch / Burger Rock	18
9.	5.44	L	Bell Valley—the Toll House	20
10.	5.44	L	Edna Wallach House	22

BOONVILLE—HIGHWAY 128 (There are no mile-markers in Boonville)

11.	R	Original Live Oak Building / Anderson Valley Brewery	26
12.	R	The McGimsey House / The Eucalyptus Trees	28
13.	L	The Grammar School / Veterans' Building & Senior Center	30
14.	L	The Track Inn / Vacant lot	32
15.	R	Boonville Business / 'SoBo' / 'Booneville'? / Gas Stations...	34
16.	R	The Live Oak Building / Central Boonville	38
17.	L	The County Fairgrounds	42
18.	R	Richmond Store / Anderson Valley Market	44
19.	L	Finney's / Ferrell's / Rossi Hardware	46
20.	R	The Boonville Lodge	50
21.	L	The Missouri House	52
22.	R	The J.T. Farrer Building	54
23.	R	The Anytime Saloon	56

BOONVILLE—LAMBERT LANE (Left off Hwy 128—opposite The Buckhorn)
24.   L at end   Lambert House / Walker House 60

BOONVILLE—HIGHWAY 128
25.   Boonville—Looking North 62
26.   Boonville—Looking South 64
27.   R   St. John's / Wiese's Valley Inn / The Buckhorn 66
28.   L   Antrum's Store / Post Office / Boonville Hotel parking lot... 70
29.   L   The Boonville Hotel 74
30.   R   The Presley House.. 78
31.   L   The Duff / Grandma June House / Center property........... 80

ANDERSON VALLEY WAY (Left at 28.02 mile-marker on Hwy 128)
32.   R   The Rose / Prather Place 84
33.   L   The Fry / Wasson-Smith House 86
34.   L   Old A.V. High Schools / A.V. Elementary School 88
35.   R   The Little White - Red schoolhouse / A.V. Museum.......... 92

HIGHWAY 128
36. Past 23.75 L   Tom Ruddock House on Ruddock Road South................. 96

PHILO—HIGHWAY 128
37. 23.00   L   Philo Schools / Baxter Winery Tasting Room / PG&E..... 100
38. 23.00   R   The Johnson Store / Lemons' Market 104
39. 22.97   L   Prather Store / Philo Pottery Inn...................................... 108

HIGHWAY 128
40. Past 22.50 L   Doc Brown's House 112
41. Past 20.16 L   The C.H. Clow House 114
42. 20.75   R   The Hulbert Ranch 116
43. 20.30   R   Shields School / Gowan property 118

SIGNAL RIDGE (Left at 20.15 mile-marker on Hwy 128 on to Greenwood Rd.
                  3½ miles to Signal Ridge. Turn left)
44. ½ mile   L & R The Pronsolino Ranch 122

HIGHWAY 128
45. 19.17   R   Day Ranch (at Philip's Hill Winery Tasting Room).......... 126
46. 18.28   R   Reilly Heights.. 128
47. 18.07   L   Counts School / Reilly property / School bell 130

CLARK ROAD (Left at 17.45 mile-marker on Hwy 128)

48.	L	Guntly / Dightman / Schenck House	134
49.	L	John Gschwend / Clark House—Oldest in the Valley	136
50.	R	Christine Landing / Kirry Ranch / Holmes Ranch	138
51.	R	Dutro's Blacksmith—beyond locked gate	142
52.	R	Christine Store—beyond locked gate	144

HIGHWAY 128

53. 17.26	R	Ed Guntly Ranch / Handley Cellars Winery	148
54. 15.14	R	John Guntly Ranch / Rhys Winery	150

WENDLING / NAVARRO—HIGHWAY 128

55. 14.50	R	Wendling School (at Wendling Road)	154
56. 14.30	R	Downtown Wendling / Navarro	156
57. 14.20	R	Mill Brickhouse / Navarro Store	158
58. 14.12	L	The Ice House	160

NAVARRO—WENDLING SODA CREEK (Right at 13.97 mile-marker on Hwy 128)

59.	R	Laurel School House	162

NAVARRO—HIGHWAY 128

60. 13.88	R	Wendling—Navarro Mill Town / The Hollow	164

THE MILE-MARKERS

Mile-markers are commonly used in rural areas to help determine where a location is set. To add to the reader's enjoyment of this book, we have attached mile markers to each location. As a result it is hoped that folks will be able to take a leisurely trip through the Valley, from Mountain House to Navarro, and discover more easily the location of each building and perhaps pull in alongside the highway to take a closer look.

The book takes the reader through the Valley along 35 miles of Highway 128, traveling in a northwesterly direction from the southeast. Therefore, when buildings and houses are described as being on the left side of the Highway, they are on the west, while those on the right are on the east side. All locations are in Mendocino, north of the county line with Sonoma, and from that point the mile-marker numbers are in descending order as you drive along. Almost all of the buildings are located exactly on mile-markers, but some are not, and in those cases it is noted where the location is in relation to the nearest mile-marker. Please note that within the town limits of Boonville there are no mile-markers, and locations are therefore described in relation to each other.

ABOUT THE AUTHORS

DONALD W. (WES) SMOOT

Wes is a native of Anderson Valley, in fact the fourth generation of his family to live here. Most of his ancestors were either ranchers or worked in the timber and logging industry. Wes' occupation with the California Department of Transportation took him out of the Valley for 12 years at one point, during which time he became interested in the history of the communities in which he lived and worked. When he returned to finish his career with the highway department in the Valley, local history became a big interest and hobby—after all it was the place he knew best. He is also one of the few remaining fluent speakers of the Anderson Valley dialect, Boontling.

Wes has been actively involved in various Valley historical projects and the Valley Museum for over twenty years and says, "This book has given me the opportunity to share my knowledge of the Valley with others and also to do further research into the Valley's rich history—I thought I knew a lot but I have learned so much more! It is my sincere hope that those who read this book will get as much enjoyment in doing so as I did in helping to assemble it."

STEVE SPARKS

Steve has a somewhat different background to that of his cowriter. In fact, to use an English expression, their backgrounds are "as different as chalk and cheese." Steve is English and grew up in that country's second largest city, Birmingham. After graduating from university he moved to the United States and traveled around taking whatever jobs he could find—these included running the bumper cars at the amusement park on the New Jersey shore to building swimming pools, making sandwiches, and working on oil rigs in Texas. He married Patty Liddy from Detroit and settled down in San Francisco in 1985, where they opened, owned, and operated one of San Francisco's busiest pubs—The Mad Dog in the Fog—for fifteen years. In 2002, deciding that it was time to "head to the hills" and escape city life and the rigors of the San Francisco bar scene, Patty and Steve moved to Anderson Valley, where, back in 1992, they had bought a small home on ten acres. Steve then threw himself into many volunteer activities that included membership of the A.V. Senior Center Board and the A.V. Historical Board, as well as organizing the A.V. Film Festival, the A.V. Animal Rescue Fundraiser, the Valley's annual Veterans Day event, and becoming head coach of the A.V. High School soccer team, along with his weekly contribution to the Anderson Valley Advertiser newspaper.

Steve's interest in history came as a result of many hours spent listening to the recollections of his maternal grandfather who was a wounded veteran of World War I. This led to him studying that war in detail at university and, several years later, becoming a member of San Francisco's World War I Society. Once in Anderson Valley, he became cofounder and de facto president of the military history book club and it was perhaps inevitable that he would become interested in local history. The germination of this book began after a meeting with local history expert Wes over lunch at the Anderson Valley Senior Center in 2011.

Steve's previous book, cowritten with County Sheriff Tom Allman and published in 2013, was entitled *Out There in the Woods* and told the true story of the extraordinary 36-day manhunt for double-murderer Aaron Bassler that took place in the Mendocino coastal forests during the fall of 2011.

Wes Smoot and Steve Sparks

Acknowledgments

Our three main "Valley History Experts":
—Donald Pardini, Eileen Pronsolino, and Pat Hulbert

Marian McAbee—for her Valley knowledge and all those cookies and cups of coffee

Patty Liddy—for all of her support and understanding as husband Steve Sparks "disappeared" to explore the Valley with Wes a few times every month.

Local Valley folks—for their knowledge, contributions, and support:
   Vicky Center
   Joanne Charles
   Christine Clark
   Mary Darling
   Jo Gowan
   Sheri Hansen
   Eva Johnson
   Bill Kimberlin
   June Lemons
   Marianne Pardini
   Donna Reilly
   Carolyn Short
   Beryl and Rubin Thomasson
   Berna Walker

Folks from further afield with Valley connections:
   Connie Mann
   Marilyn Heitz
   John and Darlyn Calvi
   Dr. George Lee

And the many other people, too numerous to mention, who contributed photographs and information as we traveled around the Valley.

The Anderson Valley Historical Society Board:
—for their financial support and constant encouragement

'Images of America—Anderson Valley' (2005):
—compiled by Sheri Hansen, Hayes Brennan, Joyce Christen, and Wes Smoot.
(a book that became known to the authors of this book as 'The Bible')

Leya Booth, Steven W. Booth, and Cyrus Wraith Walker at Genius Book Services for their excellent editing, layout, and cover art services.

Loren Doppenberg for his unique and wonderful map.

INTRODUCTION

This project began about three years ago when long-time Valley resident Wes Smoot and I were talking over lunch at the Anderson Valley Senior Center about our mutual desire to do something that might ensure that aspects of local history would be recorded and kept alive for the future generations. If at the same time we could make a little money for the Anderson Valley Historical Society and Museum by carrying out a historical project that interested us both, then that would be ideal. As a result, all profits from book sales will indeed go to that wonderful organization.

I had come to know Wes a year or so earlier, during the research for my biography of him for the "Lives and Times of Anderson Valley Folks" series I was writing at that time for the local newspaper, the Anderson Valley Advertiser. Ours is an unusual pairing on the surface—a gentleman in his early eighties, born and raised in the country, one of the few remaining speakers of the area's unique dialect, Boontling, and someone who has spent almost his entire life in the Valley; and an Englishman, 25 years younger, who did not discover Anderson Valley until 1991, having grown up in a big industrial city 6000 miles away where they speak real English! Anyway, we are linked by our respect for history and it seems to have worked. So much so that I can say without reservation that working with Wes on this project has been a very rewarding experience indeed—he is a true gentleman, one with a fine sense of humor, and someone who accepts the need for change almost as much as he reveres the past.

During that discussion at the Senior Center we came up with the idea of working on a study of the many old buildings in the Valley, in the form of both brief histories and also photographs of them from the past and today, or of what is now there where they once stood. Wes' knowledge of the area is amongst the best of the Valley's "old-timers" and this expertise has been the basis of the writing and recording of the history presented in the book, along with those recollections of a few other Valley folks whose input has been vital to this endeavor. Our particular appreciation goes to these three "Valley history experts"—Donald Pardini, Eileen Pronsolino, and Pat Hulbert, each of whom we have spoken to at length about these buildings and homes.

Very early on it was decided to only include homes and buildings that were at least 70 years old, from before the early 1940s, and, just as importantly, to be included we had to have photographs of them taken from that time. We worked from there all the way back virtually to the initial discovery of the Valley by white folks in the early 1850s—the earliest photograph we came across is from 1856. The decision of which buildings and homes to include was always going to be decided by these main criteria, as Wes and I drove up and down the Valley many, many times, taking current photographs of those buildings or what is there now. We would then sit down at the dining table at Wes' home in Boonville to discuss the histories of each of them and write the texts. As I mentioned earlier, this took about three years, during which time we met perhaps twice a month, sometimes more often. In fact, if I don't get my dose of Wes' country calmness and effortless humor every week or so, my wife Patty thinks I start to return to the ways of an impatient "bright-lighter"! (That's "city-dweller" in Boontling).

We ended up with about 120 possible buildings—far too many for the kind of publication we had in mind; one that would be enjoyed by both those with a casual interest in history as well as the more keen followers, and perhaps a few Valley visitors too. Over time we found that getting old photographs of a number of these—remember the pictures had to be taken before the mid-1940s—was not an easy task, or certainly not one we could attempt given our wish to finish this book before I became a senior myself! As a result we reduced the total to about 80, of which we eventually decided on 'the best' 60 homes and buildings, based mostly at that point on the quality of the old photographs. All of them that made the book have *Then and Now* photographs, and are accompanied by a brief history, provided by either homeowners or our panel of experts. It should be noted that as often as possible the current photographs were taken from the same spot as the old ones, but this was not always possible, primarily due to too many trees being in the way to get a corresponding picture. In those cases, getting as near as possible, yet still making a relevant comparison, was the option we took.

Finally, I should point out that the histories are intentionally brief. There is no doubt a more detailed account to be written on each of the selected locations but that is perhaps for others to do and was not an intention of this project. The book is not an historical tome; it is aimed at the general public and will hopefully provide an easy, flowing read, while at the same time be informative and even entertaining to everyone who buys a copy. In today's 'I need to be entertained' society, the study of history needs to provide that, certainly if it is to continue as a significant source of interest for future generations.

Wes and I sincerely hope you enjoy the 'journey'…
Keep turning the pages of history,
Steve Sparks
May 2014

THE VIEW FROM BURGER ROCK AND THE DISCOVERY OF ANDERSON VALLEY

Burger Rock can be viewed from near to the junction of Highway 128 and Highway 253, by looking ½ mile in a southeasterly direction. The Rock is situated on what is today the Johnson Ranch and, as you will read, has a very significant part to play in the historical background of the Valley.

The first photograph shows the view of the Valley that would be very similar to that facing those first settlers at the time of the Valley's discovery in 1851. It was taken in 1885 from that same observation point at which they would have stood—later known as Burger Rock.

The second picture was taken in December 2013 when, with the kind permission of Eva Johnson and family, who have owned the property for many years, the authors Wes Smoot and Steve Sparks made their way up to this special place. It is believed that this most recent photograph is the only photograph ever taken from Burger Rock in wintertime as it can be quite an inhospitable place with high winds, and the sheer drops are not one for the faint-hearted at that time of year. This photograph features the Anderson Valley Brewery in the foreground, the Penny Royal cheese factory centre-left, the heart of Boonville upper-center, and a large number of vines on the east side of town, dormant for the winter.

Two very similar stories tell of the first white folks to discover the Valley. According to Lyman L. Palmer in the book 'Mendocino County History 1880' (written at that time), in 1851 when Walter Anderson migrated into this country 'he made his way down the long open ridge where this big rock stood and looked down upon the valley. Below and before him outspread a fertile valley fifteen miles long and about two miles in width, which he rightly judged could easily be converted into a paradise and a home such as he had never found in all his peregrinations throughout the length and breadth of the land and he determined to bring his journey to a close, in this almost vale of Cashmere.'

Anderson Valley acquired its name from this same Walter Anderson while the Rock acquired its name sometime in the late 1800s from the landowner at the time, Renus Burger. However, Walter was not the first white person to see the Valley as a number of folks have incorrectly assumed...

Anderson Valley from Burger Rock, 1885

Anderson Valley from Burger Rock, Winter 2013

Valley historian, Eleanor Clow, did extensive research into the subject, along with others including our own Valley expert, Pat Hulbert. Eleanor reported a similar tale of discovery, one that does not disagree with the first story. In fact it actually adds greatly to it and most importantly reveals who first saw the Valley…

"This rock has significant historical background. It was in the fall of 1851 when Walter Anderson, along with his family, migrated into a small settlement called Oat Valley (Author's note—Oat Valley is on Highway 128 just outside present day Cloverdale, in Sonoma County). There they made camp and his son William Anderson and two stepsons, named Henry and Isaac Beeson, decided to go hunt for some meat. At some point they wounded an elk and while in search for the animal their course led them to a stony ledge that looked down upon a fertile valley that was almost beyond belief.

"They continued down into the valley and lingered there for several days before returning to Oat Valley. They explained to the rest of the family that they had found a "big meadow, and it was 'like a garden of Eden.'

"Their father, Walter Anderson, hooked up a wagon and they returned to this newly discovered land. Traveling down the long open ridge where this big Rock stood they looked down upon the valley. 'Below and before them outspread a fertile valley fifteen miles long and about two miles in width, which Mr. Anderson rightly judged could easily be converted into a paradise and a home such as he had never found in all his peregrinations throughout the length and breadth of the land and he determined to bring his journey to a close.'—Lyman Palmer's account in 1880.

"However as they were preparing to construct a small log shelter for the winter, the local Indians arrived and, remembering a previous incident in Lake County with Indians, they decided to retreat to a location in the Dry Creek Valley, west of present day Healdsburg. Then in the spring of 1852 the Anderson family returned to this valley that was to become their home. By making this move they became the first settlers in this valley and it was named Anderson Valley and has been called such ever since."

AUTHORS' NOTES

- In our opinion, given that the distance from Oat Valley to Boonville is about 27 miles by road today, this hunting trip taken by the three young men across difficult terrain, over never before discovered territory, would have been a far greater distance and perhaps would have taken a month or so at least, one way. There is also some discrepancy with another account that has the Andersons living in Lake County immediately before settling in the Valley, not Sonoma. It has proved difficult to clarify this definitively. However, it is known that when the Anderson Party returned to settle in 1852 they built their family home west of the current high school, beneath the hills and forests.

- The first settlement was called The Corners and was located where Highway 128 and Highway 253 meet today. By 1864, Alonzo Kendall had built the Hotel a mile or so further north and changed the named to Kendall City. As for the name 'Boonville', following

Kendall's departure for the coast in the late 1860's, the local people decided to change the name of the settlement from Kendall City to the new name of Boonville, after the postmaster W.W. Boone. A few folks think that for a time it was 'Booneville' but most people do not. Based on our research, the only time the name could have been officially 'Booneville' was from the time the name was changed from Kendall City, in 1867, to when it appears as 'Boonville' in official records in 1884. After further research, it was found that three of the other (six) such named towns around the country are spelled 'Booneville' with the middle 'e', but the other three are 'Boonville,' without that middle 'e'. These include the one in Missouri, not far from where W.W. Boone had originally come from before heading to California, and one that was named after the sons of Daniel Boone, who were the second cousins of W.W. Boone. (See related comments in #25 and #28.)

In 'The History of Mendocino County, CA', originally published in 1880, Boonville appears with an 'e' in it throughout the whole document – see the interesting excerpt in italics below:

1876. The Board of Supervisors established the following as the' legal distances from Ukiah':-

Booneville	*20 miles*	
Christine	*32 miles*	(Clark Road, Gschwend Road, Guntly Road area in 2014)
Hopland	*14 miles*	
McDonalds	*22 miles*	(2014's Mountain House – junction of Hwy 128 and Hopland Rd)

In conclusion we believe that for almost 20 years after the name of the town was changed in 1867, 'Boonville' was frequently written in two different ways, although officially it was probably always spelled without a middle 'e'. This definitive spelling of the town came from a mistake made by a clerk compiling the Grand Register of Mendocino County in 1866 at the County Records office. This person entered W.W. Boone's name as W.W. Boon, leaving off the 'e', and also misspelling his middle name as Waitsell instead of Waightstall. Shortly thereafter, the folks living in the small town in Anderson Valley decided to name their town after local resident W.W. Boone, changing it from Kendall City. Based on this incorrect spelling in the record books, it was therefore registered as 'Boonville.' This mistake was compounded in the 1870 Census where there appears a further 'Boon' spelling for W.W.'s last name.

In the ensuing years, many folks, including some of those writing history books such as the aforementioned 'A History of Mendocino County,' in 1880, who knew of the Boone name, would spell the town's name as 'Booneville,' with the middle 'e'. However, it would seem that by 1884, with official records sticking with 'Boonville' by that time, the alternative spelling ceased to be used by anyone and the name has stayed that way ever since – well almost – there were a couple of unofficial and odd instances in the late 1950s (see #15 – page 37).

An Anderson Valley Journey

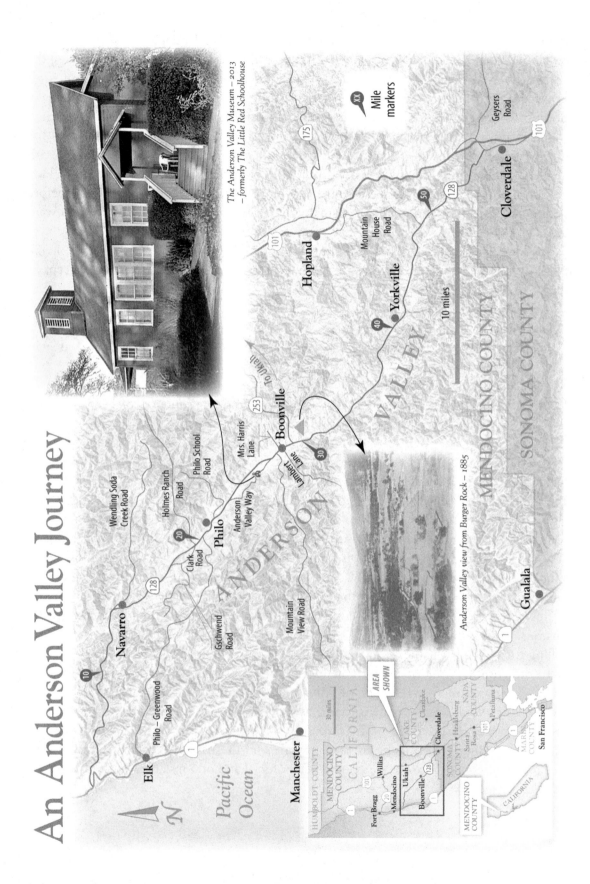

The Anderson Valley Museum — 2013
— formerly The Little Red Schoolhouse

Mile markers

Anderson Valley view from Burger Rock — 1885

Pacific Ocean

Elk

Navarro

Manchester

Philo

Boonville

Hopland

Yorkville

Cloverdale

Gualala

Philo – Greenwood Road

Wending Soda Creek Road

Holmes Ranch Road

Philo School Road

Clark Road

Gschwend Road

Mountain View Road

Anderson Valley Way

Mrs. Harris Lane

Lambert Lane

Mountain House Road

Geysers Road

to Ukiah

ANDERSON VALLEY

MENDOCINO COUNTY

SONOMA COUNTY

10 miles

AREA SHOWN

CALIFORNIA

MENDOCINO COUNTY

HUMBOLDT COUNTY

LAKE COUNTY

Clearlake

NAPA COUNTY

SONOMA COUNTY

MARIN COUNTY

Cloverdale

Healdsburg

Santa Rosa

Petaluma

San Francisco

Willits

Ukiah

Fort Bragg

Mendocino

Boonville

30 miles

HIGHWAY 128

1. MOUNTAIN HOUSE
Hwy 128: 48.50 mile marker—on the left

The Mountain House Hotel (1a) was located behind where the large family house stood on the west side of the highway. The hotel burned down completely in 1898. Prior to that it served as a layover and stage stop for people traveling north from Cloverdale to Ukiah and Willits and beyond, on what was at the time Highway 101. The highway remained as such until around 1930 when a new highway was constructed from Cloverdale to Hopland along the Russian River—the current Highway 101, and the road to Mountain House became Highway 28, later becoming Highway 128.

At the Mountain House the road split, one way took travelers to Hopland, the other went to the coast via Anderson Valley and was known as "McDonald's-to-the-Sea" for the simple reason that the McDonald family owned the ranch where the hotel was located. In 1900, the McDonald Ranch was purchased by Mr. Ed Haehl and he built the big house that stands next to the highway today, shown here not long after its construction had been completed (1b).

In 1910, Mr. Haehl sold the ranch and house to E. Bowlen Hiatt, his wife Mary, and their children. When Bowlen Hiatt passed away the ranch was left to the three children, Maxwell, George Washington, and Gertrude Hiatt with Mary Hiatt as life tenant. Mary lived in the house until she passed away on her 87th birthday on December 26th, 1959. Mary's daughter Gertrude continued to live in the house until she passed on in 1960.

In the meantime, G. W. Hiatt and his wife Mabel and two daughters lived in a small house across the road from the big house until the ranch was sold in 1972. Since that time the house has passed through several hands and became a bed and breakfast for a time. It has undergone major renovations inside although the exterior looks very similar to the original (1c).

1a. McDonald's-to-the-Sea Hotel, 1890s

1b. Mountain House, Early 1900s

1c. Mountain House, 2011

2. THE 'OLD CHATHAM' RANCH

Hwy 128: 47.19 mile marker—on the right, up hill

(This house is at the end of a private driveway and cannot be visited.
It appears in this book simply to show the kind of buildings that were once built
in the Valley and, in this case, how they have been wonderfully preserved.)

This house (2b), situated above the highway on the Haehl grade, a little over a mile west of the Mountain House, is generally regarded as the most elegant-looking house for its age in the Yorkville / Mountain House area. The house was built in 1856 and was originally owned by W.H. Cook. There were three or four different owners before the Hunt Family sold the house and 120 acres to Richard and Helen Gilman in August of 1894. It is shown here in the late 1890s (2a). The Gilmans did extensive remodeling to the house but never disturbed the structure. In the following years the ranch and house were sold to several different families, one of which was the Shortridge family sometime in the late 1920s or early 1930s, followed by the Rainoldi's, the Weeks', and the Sanders'.

In 1979, the ranch was sold to Dr. George Lee and his family from the Bay Area. Dr. Lee had originally planned to tear down the old house and build a new one just to the southeast of the present location. However, after looking into the past history of the old house and ranch, Dr. Lee decided that he could not destroy this historical site so he carried out some remodeling, added a room or two, and now there is once again a beautiful home on the ranch. The name 'Old Chatham' Ranch was selected by the Lee children, commemorating the town, Old Chatham, in which they were born in eastern New York state.

2a. The Gilman House, Late 1890s

2b. The Old Chatham Ranch, 2013

3. GASKILL SCHOOL HOUSE
Hwy 128: 45.99 mile marker—on the right

The little one-room schoolhouse (3b) sits vacant alongside Highway 128, as it has done so since its closure in 1947—when the State mandated that all schools must have running water and flush toilets. Flush toilets were the one thing that this school did not have, and together with the fact that after four students graduated from the eighth grade in 1946 there were only three students left, this resulted in the County's decision to close the school and consolidate it with the Anderson Valley school district.

The schoolhouse was originally located about two miles northwest of this location, across the road a ways from the W.I. Ingram house and adjacent to Dog Town at the 44 mile marker on Highway 128. The school was approved by the County of Mendocino on November 21st, 1860 and was number #6 in the County.

It was moved to its current location in 1926 (3a) and was placed on property donated to the school district by Silas E. Gaskill whereby it acquired the name Gaskill School. Throughout its lifespan the school only had one teacher at a time, teaching all grades one through eight. The schoolhouse stood vacant from 1947 to 2012 when the Johnson (Stanley) Ranch property was purchased by a farmer and rancher named Adam Hyde. After learning the history of the school, Mr. Hyde is currently in the process of attempting to restore the building back to its original state and give it new life in the years to come. If you are driving along Highway 128, the view from the road (at 45.99 mile marker) is that shown in photograph 3c.

Note: Co-author of this book, Wes Smoot, attended the school at this location from 1938-46, 1st through 8th grade, before moving, in September 1946, to the high school in Boonville, situated where the District Office currently sits—see #34.

3a. Gaskill School, 1926

3b. Abandoned Gaskill School, 2013

3c. Abandoned School from Highway 128, 2011

4. THE MORROW HOUSE
Hwy 128: 44.75 mile marker—on the left

As near as can be determined, the Morrow House was built around 1874 and was finally dismantled around 2006, a span of some 132 years. When it was torn down, a piece of newspaper was found fastened to one of the walls dated 1874.

Sometime in the 1920s, the house and ranch were bought by Mr. J. H. Morrow, who was the purchasing agent for Contra Costa County in Pittsburg, California. In 1930 (4a), the house was rented by the Smoot family who made it their home until 1947, and this is where co-author Wes Smoot lived until he was 15 years old.

Mr. Ray Smoot drove the school bus from Yorkville to Boonville for the Anderson Valley School District for 19 years from 1928 until his death in 1947. After Ray Smoot's passing, the Smoots moved to Boonville, and in early 1948 the Hill family from Cloverdale moved into the house. Mr. Hill took on the job of running the Morrow sheep ranch for several years until leaving and settling at the Ingram ranch in 1959 (see #5).

After the Morrows passed away they left the ranch and house to their son, Keith Morrow, who rarely visited the property. In 1999 or thereabouts, he sold the ranch to a winery owner and shortly after that the house was torn down. There now remains a vacant spot and a dilapidated trailer where this old house stood for so many years (4b).

4a. Morrow House, circa 1936

4b. Derelict shack, 2012

5. W.I. (IRVIN) & E.R. (RUTH) INGRAM HOUSE / HILL RANCH

Hwy 128: 44.01 mile marker—on the right

Irvin and Ruth (Hiatt) Ingram purchased 680 acres of land with a house and barns from James McCausland in September, 1911 for the sum of $5,000. Ruth is shown in front of the house a year or so later (5a), with her mother, Elizabeth Hiatt, and two of her brothers, Theophilus Lee and Charlie, who was the local postmaster at the time—see #6.

Irvin was not only a great rancher but was also a skilled and experienced teamster and expertly drove a team of horses and a wagon. Irvin's wife, Ruth was a very good cook and was well known in the area for always having cakes, pies, and cookies to nibble on.

Irvin and Ruth had one daughter, named Ruby. She married a gentleman from Cloverdale by the name of Fred Vadon and in July 1962 the ranch was inherited by Ruby. Two years later, on July 31, 1964, the ranch was deeded to Ruby and Fred's daughter and son-in-law, Ruth Marie and her husband Harold Hill, who had moved there from the Morrow House in 1959.

In 1965, the old Ingram House needed some extensive repairs so it was torn down and a new house was constructed in the same location (5b). This house is now the home of Ruth Marie Hill and her son (the great grandson of Irvin Ingram), Jim Hill, who runs the ranch to this day with sheep, goats, and Christmas trees, among the many activities that keep Jim busy—he is also the current president of the Anderson Valley Historical Society. (Several times a year—Chrismas, Easter, etc.—Jim places appropriate decorations in the pastures that are clearly visibile from the highway.)

Lee HIATT - ELIZABETH LEDFORD HIATT -RUTH HIATT INGRAM- CHAS. HIATT

5a. Ingram Ranch House, 1911

5b. Hill Ranch House, 2014

6. YORKVILLE POST OFFICES

2nd Yorkville Post Office. Hwy 128: 38.50 mile marker—on the right

The post office in this area has had five different locations and, for the purposes of this book, we shall cover them in geographical order (as the reader travels north along Highway 128), not in chronological order. The photographs refer to only the second of these five post offices.

The Yorkville post office was moved to its 3rd location, a spot in White Hall, about three miles south of where the 2nd post office had stood for many years. This was in the store owned by Allie Prather, and where in more recent times the Yorkville Mini-Mart was located (at mile marker 41.29). Allie added a room onto her store, made it into a post office, and became the postmistress. The Yorkville Post Office kept that name and so its move to the new location resulted in White Hall's "disappearance" as a town. It became a part of Yorkville and the road signs were changed indicating this new location as Yorkville. Other folks who ran the post office over the years include Emmabelle Withrell, Wesley Hulbert, Claude and Lou Rose, and Debbie Johnson.

In 1978, another location change was made when postmaster Leo Marcott and his wife Barbara sold the store to Rubin and Marie Thomasson. Leo wanted to remain as postmaster but the Thomassons wanted to remodel the store so Leo had the post office moved directly across the highway and into a room in his own house, thus becoming Yorkville's 4th post office location.

In 1990 a new building was constructed on the Hulbert property, on land donated by Austin and Silvia Hulbert, just over a mile to the north on Highway 128 (at mile marker 40.24). This new building today serves as a multifunction building for the Yorkville community, becoming the new post office (5th) as well as a fire station and community center.

To cover the first two Yorkville post offices, the traveler must continue to drive further north to around the 38.50 mile marker, and we must go back in history quite a ways as we refer to the photographs shown here…

In 1889, E. M. Hiatt retired as postmaster of the original Yorkville post office that had been located in the front of the Hiatt Hotel on the Yorkville Ranch property—see #7. After his retirement, the post office was moved to a building to the south of the Hotel (6a). It was here that E.M. Hiatt's son, Charles Hiatt★ (in photograph 6b) became the postmaster, a position he remained in for 48 years until a devastating flood in the winter of 1937-38 washed the post office down Rancheria Creek, never to be seen again.

★ For anyone counting, Charlie Hiatt is the only person to appear in two photographs in this book! He is also in the group standing in front of the Ingram Ranch in photograph 5a.

Located directly behind the old post office was a house where the postmaster lived. This house survived the floods and is where Duane Ornbaun now lives (6c). Duane is the son of the late Pete Ornbaun who was foreman of the Yorkville Ranch for many years.

6a. 2nd Yorkville
Post Office, 1889

6b. Charlie Hiatt,
Postmaster 1889–1937

6c. Duane Ornbaun House,
2011

7. YORKVILLE HOTEL / MCDONALD'S-TO-THE-SEA HIGHWAY
Hwy 128: 38.33 mile marker—on the right

In the early 1860s, Elijah M. Hiatt and his wife Elizabeth came to the little valley that would later become Yorkville. In 1867, they purchased land from a close friend of theirs, Richard York, and developed the first sheep ranch in the area. Elijah then purchased other parcels of land adjoining his so that by June, 1909 when he died he had a ranch of 6,000 acres.

The land on top of the mountain is still known as Hiatt Mountain. In 1867, Elijah built a large house for his wife and family, and soon after that he turned it into a hotel (7a—taken around 1888). Just inside the front door of the hotel was the first post office of what was to be known as Yorkville. Close by the hotel he built a large barn and a blacksmith shop.

The ranch has been broken down into smaller parcels and sold, and today the house is owned by Mr. Ron Rice and is surrounded by only about 40 acres, a number of which are planted with olive trees. The old house has undergone some major reconstruction and was moved back from the highway about 20 feet (7b) but it continues to remain a well-known landmark in the community.

The hotel served as a stage stop (7c) as well as a place to change horses for either the trip on to Boonville, on the road called McDonald's-to-the-Sea (now Highway 128—photograph 7d) and points north, or the journey to Hermitage, Mountain House, and other points east and south. The hotel also served meals to stage passengers and was a place to stay overnight before continuing on their journeys. (The second Yorkville post office was constructed on the ground just out of photograph 7c to the right—see photograph 6a.)

Elijah Hiatt and Richard York wanted to give a name to the small valley where they lived, but each of them wanted it named after himself. In order to decide this dilemma they played a game of cards with the winner receiving the honor of having the area named after him. The loser of the game would become the postmaster. Undoubtedly Richard York won the game and Yorkville was founded, while E. M. Hiatt became the local postmaster (see #6). There never was a Hiattville!

The hotel was converted back into a family house and has changed ownership several times. At one point the property nearby the ranch, on Elk Horn Road, was owned by Frank Delenbal from Oakland. Pat Hulbert's father and his parents moved there in 1927 and it was called the Diamond D Ranch, and her grandfather, Arthur Hulbert, drove the school bus. Pat remembers, "Pete and Helen Ornbaun lived at what had been the Yorkville Hotel when Duane Ornbaun was a child. Duane now lives in the house nearby, where the 2nd Yorkville Post Office was. Duane's sister, Bonnie, was my best friend and I had many sleepovers in the old hotel. It was called the "Y" Ranch for a long time due to the huge "Y" on the old barn there."

(Note: for your information as you travel along, the next building in the book is not until you reach the outskirts of Boonville, about 8 miles further north on Highway 128)

7a. The Yorkville Hotel, circa 1870s

7b. Former Yorkville Hotel, 2012

7c. McDonald's-to-the-Sea Highway, Late 1860s

7d. Highway 128 at Yorkville Ranch, 2012

Highway 253

(Right off Highway 128 at sign to Ukiah)

8. RENUS BURGER HOUSE / BURGER ROCK
Turn right (east) off Hwy 128 on to Hwy 253, 600'—on the right

The Renus and Elizabeth Burger house was located on the south side of Ukiah road, Highway 253, about 200 yards east of Highway 128. It was a very large house and was the home to Renus and Elizabeth and their four children—Hale, Louise Jane, Alex Nathon, and Georgia Pearl Burger.

The house was built sometime around the late 1890s (8a) on a ranch consisting of around 2,000 acres. From this family and ranch came the name of a very prominent landmark that overlooks the Valley and provides one its most iconic views—Burger Rock, the point from which some compelling photographs of Anderson Valley have been taken. It is the high point directly to the southeast of the present Johnson ranch on highway 253, and the edge of it can be seen in the background of this photograph.

After the passing of Renus, his wife Elizabeth remained in the home until her passing in 1948. The house was then rented to several different people and it fell into a state of disrepair, so much so that the house was torn down by Fay Deeley in the mid-1960s and the remainder of the ranch was purchased by Floyd Johnson, whose wife Eva and their descendants continue to own and operate the Johnson Ranch today. Where the house once stood is now a vacant spot in a large sheep pasture, with Burger Rock standing proudly in the background (8b).

8a. Renus Burger House, circa 1900

8b. Pastures on the Johnson Ranch, 2013

9. BELL VALLEY—THE TOLL HOUSE

Hwy 253: 5.44 mile marker—on the left

*(The photographs for this location were taken from private land across the road
that is not open to the public.)*

The Toll House is a large house built in Bell Valley, about six miles out of Boonville on Highway 253. It was constructed by the Millers in the late 1800s and the photographs shown here give an overview of Bell Valley with the house in the center (9a).

The name "The Toll House" comes from the late 1860s. Around that time, Mr. John Gschwend, who had a lumber mill business at the northwest end of Anderson Valley (see #49), started to build a road over the hill from Boonville to just south of Ukiah with money initially collected from private subscriptions to subsidize the road-building. When such financing failed he completed the road himself, using horses pulling a "reversing single gang turn plow" that allowed the dirt to be turned in the same direction when ploughed in either direction. Gschwend needed the road to get from his mill in the Valley to the market in Ukiah. Other folks obviously used the road too and so in 1868 he secured a permit from the county supervisors to establish this road as a toll road to recoup some of his investment. The gate for toll payments was in Bell Valley, in front of what was to be known as the "Old Miller House" that in later years was to be called "The Toll House."

Bell Valley was the home of many hop fields and was a central location for surrounding sheep ranchers to drive their sheep to be sheared. The small area where the Toll House sits is the location where the strange language, or rather dialect, called "Boontling" was given its birth. In later years the house underwent some major reconstruction and today it remains not only a very lovely old house but is also a well-known landmark throughout the region (9b).

9a. The Toll House / Bell Valley, Late 1800s

9b. The Toll House / Bell Valley, 2013

10. EDNA WALLACH HOME
Hwy 253: 5.44 mile marker—on the left
(This old home can be viewed primarily via the Toll House property,
and permission to pass through should be obtained beforehand.)

The William and Edna Wallach house is located just behind the famed Toll House on Highway 253, about six miles east of Boonville. The house was built with lumber sawed by the old Clow sawmill that was located on the west side of the highway, across the Valley from the Shorty Rawles ranch, which today is the Lichen Winery, situated about halfway between Boonville and Philo.

The house was built sometime in the late 1860s or early 1870s (10a - pictured in the early 1890s). The lumber to build it was hauled up to Bell Valley by a wagon and a four-horse team. That very wagon used to haul the lumber is still on display at the Mendocino County Fair and Apple Show grounds in Boonville, where it has been restored and painted.

After William passed away, Edna remained there for the rest of her life. Edna seldom went anywhere but she loved to have friends and neighbors over to her home. She also spent a lot of time talking over the phone to different folks down in Anderson Valley and sharing various tales of folks using a strange dialect that the Wallachs and their neighbors had started to develop.

During the war years, Edna ran an aircraft identification station at her place. She was instrumental in leading the authorities to find the fated China Clipper aircraft that crashed just behind her property in January, 1943. The crash killed all 19 people and crew aboard. Edna tried, on several occasions, to tell the authorities where the plane went down but they would not listen to her until finally someone decided to go look where she told them, and sure enough there it was.

Since Edna passed away there has been no one living in the old house and it has slowly decayed (10b). The ranch has changed owners several times during the past years and the brush and shrubbery has grown up around the house to a point where it is no longer visible until one is very close by. Nevertheless, it has left its mark because this is where the Wallachs, Singleys, Millers, and McSpaddens were significantly instrumental in the development of the region's unique and increasingly rare language, known as Boontling, of which co-author Wes Smoot is one of the few remaining speakers.

10a. Edna Wallach House, Early 1890s

10b. Abandoned house, 2012

BOONVILLE—HIGHWAY 128

(There are no mile-markers in Boonville)

11. ORIGINAL LIVE OAK BUILDING / ANDERSON VALLEY BREWERY

Hwy 128: about 100' northwest of junction with Hwy 253
—on the right, opposite Hutsell Lane

In the early 1920s, with the rapid increase in the number of automobiles, trucks, and farm machinery, there became a much greater demand for a place to repair these items. On the outskirts of Boonville at that time there was a large barn that stood next to the road on the northeast corner of the junction of the Ukiah road and the main highway through town. This barn belonged to Charles Albert Tarwater, or as he was better known CAT, who decided to convert the barn into a repair and a blacksmith shop. It was an instant success.

By 1924, the repair business had grown to the point where CAT needed help so he hired Glenn McAbee, who was a good mechanic and welder, along with Sam Fitch, who was well-versed in the blacksmith trade. This made a trio of expert repairmen. CAT named his successful business "The Live Oak Garage," surrounded as it was by those so-named trees. The unique photograph (11a) was taken during the winter of 1924-25, one that saw significant snowfall in the Valley. A year later CAT needed to expand his business so he constructed a new building in town—see #16.

Today, the spot of the original Live Oak Garage is on the grounds of the Anderson Valley Brewery—in an area on the edge of the brewery's disc golf course. How times have changed! (11b).

11a. Original Live Oak Building, 1925

11b. Anderson Valley Brewery at Highway 128/253 junction, 2013

12. THE MCGIMSEY HOUSE / THE EUCALYPTUS TREES

Hwy 128: about 300' northwest of junction with Hwy 253—on the right

The old house standing behind the twin eucalyptus trees was located about 100 yards northwest of the junction with Highway 253 and on the east side of Highway 128. It is unknown exactly when the house was built, by Beth Tuttle's grandparents, however this photograph (12a) is from the 1930s, and it is a known fact that the two trees standing in front of it were planted in 1874 and they were about 6 feet tall at that time.

The house has been rented out a number of times in the past and at one time it sat on land owned by Mr. Herb Singley. After his passing the property was purchased by the Anderson Valley Brewing Company and it remains in their hands today.

The old house fell into a dilapidated condition and was torn down sometime in the mid-1970s. Now at the grand old age of 140 years, the twin eucalyptus trees stand beside the highway like two sentries welcoming people to Anderson Valley (12b).

12a. McGimsey House, circa 1930s

12b. The Eucalyptus Trees, 2012

13. THE GRAMMAR SCHOOL / VETERANS' BUILDING & SENIOR CENTER
On the left—at signs for the Senior Center

What was once the Boonville grammar school is at what is now the Veterans' Building / Senior Center, located at the south end of Boonville.

However… Going back to the beginning, the first school of any kind in the Valley was a one-room log cabin located near where the present CalTrans yard is currently situated, at the north end of Boonville on the west side of Highway 128 as you leave town. This school was built in 1858 and was a private school, which was Anderson Valley's grammar school. It was not referred to by its Boonville name until at least 1867.

Over a period of years, and as the population increased, another school building was constructed on land now the home of the Veterans' Building, but situated some distance in front of the present building, closer to the main road. Then, in 1900, that building was dismantled and the present building was built as the grammar school (13a). This was around the same time that the school at the north end of town was closed down.

By 1928, the school population had grown to about 60 pupils and the teacher, Miss Blanche Brown, decided that it was too much for her to adequately teach all eight grades by herself and that it was not fair to the students. She approached the Mendocino County School Superintendent in Ukiah and explained the problem to him.

As a result of her efforts, the following year, when the old Yorkville School closed due to lack of students, that building was dismantled and the lumber hauled to Boonville to build another room onto the south side of the grammar school. The classes were then divided and other teachers, Hazel Nobles and Wilda Brizell, were hired to ease the teaching load. (Blanche Brown later moved to Con Creek School, in what is now the A.V. Museum, and she later taught the 8th grade when it was moved into a corner room at the high school situated across the street. She retired in 1948).

In the early 1950s a new elementary school was built about a mile north of town, alongside the site of the high school (see #34), and the Boonville grammar school was closed for good. After its closure the school district decided to sell the building and grounds to the County of Mendocino. This is when the County established the old building as a Veterans' Memorial Building. The American Legion Post #385 now had room to hold their meetings, dances, dinners, and parties and a fun time was had by all for many years until numbers dwindled. Today, the veterans hold their meetings there but few other activities in their name.

In the late 1970s, the county moved the local Justice Court room into the building. Then, in 1980, the north room of the building was enlarged and the Anderson Valley Senior Citizens moved their operation into this space—perfect for their lunches and dinners. By the late 1980s, the Courts had moved to Ukiah and Fort Bragg, and today the building remains as a Veterans' Building and a thriving Senior Citizens and Community Center, hosting many events and being available for rent for various special occasions, although it is operated under the jurisdiction of the County (13b).

13a. Boonville Grammar School, Early 1900s

13b. The Veterans' Building, 2013

14. THE TRACK INN
On the left—just past the Fairgrounds

Just past the Fairgrounds' parking lot, there is a vacant lot where once stood one of the three busy bars in the town of Boonville during the pre-World War II years. The bar was called The Track Inn and was built in 1937 by a man named Ralph Kunzler, who ran the bar for several years.

The building not only housed the bar but it also had a pool room, a poker room, a restaurant, a barbershop, and a beauty salon. In the 1940s and early 1950s, when the lumber industry was booming, the bar was so crowded, particularly during the County Fair, that sometimes they would open a little beer bar on the outside of the south side of the bar to take care of the crowd (14a).

However, by the mid-1960s, the timber industry was in decline and the workers moved on, the result of which was a drop-off in business to such a degree that the bar was closed, and soon afterwards the entire building was closed down.

In the early 1980s, property owner Delmer June had the building torn down. Today it remains vacant, a place where the grass grows and the ghosts of Valley drinking folks can sometimes be heard (14b).

(The house in the background is the home of Valley resident of seventy-five-plus years and perhaps its most knowledgeable historian, Donald Pardini, and his wife Marianne.)

14a. The Track Inn, circa 1940s

14b. Vacant Lot, 2013

15. BOONVILLE BUSINESSES / 'SOBO' / 'BOONEVILLE' / THE BOONVILLE GAS STATIONS

On the right, as you enter the business district from the south

The first photograph (15a) shows the downtown Boonville scene looking north in the early 1930s. On the right side of the road is the Live Oak Building owned by C.A. Tarwater, and further down the street is the Bivins grocery store—later to become, in order, Zittleman's, Mary Jane's Place, The Smiling Deer, The Soundbite, and today's Lauren's Restaurant. Farther on can be seen Richmond Market and its gas pumps, then The Boonville Lodge, and on towards the end is the J.T. Farrer store. On the left side just out of the shot is the Albert Ferrell gas station and hardware store, later to become Rossi's Hardware. This section of downtown became a real boomtown in the 1950s, with the Mannix Building, Tindall's Market, which was home to the post office, and many others (15b).

The Tindall grocery store was owned and operated by Maurice Tindall and his wife, Alice, for several years until they leased it to Carl Rynerson and his wife, Rose. After running the store for a year or so, they closed down, never opening again. Upstairs in the Mannix Building was an office where Homer Mannix began the local "Anderson Valley Advertiser" newspaper in the 1950s, and of which he was the owner and editor for many years. The lower level of the Mannix Building consisted of an appliance store, a hardware store, a Ford automobile dealership, and a beauty salon run by Beatrice Mannix, Homer's wife. Later on, when Mannix was appointed Justice Court Judge, he opened a courtroom too—that was in the Veterans' Building just down the street (see #13).

By the late 1980s, those businesses had all folded, the post office had moved across the street to its present location, and a fire had burned the Mannix Building to the ground. A vacant lot stood there for many years. In the photograph taken late in 2013 (15c), we can see that this vacant lot is undergoing quite a renovation. In the picture we have the "All that Good Stuff" gift store that is situated where Tindall's Market once stood, and proudly displays the original "Tindall's Market" sign on the front of the building. Many locals now refer to this whole section of town as "SoBo"—South Boonville. Also, directly behind where the Mannix Building once stood, to the left of the gift store, is where Amanda Hiatt's beauty / hair salon is located, along with Steve Wood's architecture office and the SoBo yoga studio.

BOONVILLE GAS STATIONS

It is reckoned that through the years from 1920 to the present time there have been eight gasoline stations within the town limits of Boonville, the majority of them in the area of town discussed above. Starting with the south end of town there was…

#1 was the Union Station on the south corner of Haehl Street opened by John B.E. Ashford in the early 1950s and later run by Eddie Ball and then Bob Sanders (Leo and Edna's son), before Jeff and Carolyn Short took over in the early 1960s and ran it for many, many years.

#2 was on the north corner of Haehl Street, known as The Flying A (a Shell station) and was owned by Bill Presley at one time, and today is the firehouse.

#3 was on the forecourt of the Live Oak Garage (#16).

#4 was the John Rossi station across the street from the Live Oak Building that was run for a time by Bill Holcomb.

#5 was in the front of the Richmond Grocery store (today's A.V. Market).

#6 was next to the Boonville Lodge, and was owned by Johnnie Clark for quite a while.

#7 was the J.T. Farrer station at the north side of the J.T. Farrer store—now Paysanne, an ice cream store.

#8 is the only one still in operation today—at the Redwood Drive-In.

15a. Downtown Boonville, 1930s

15b. Boonville 'Boomtown', 1952

15c. 'SoBo' (South Boonville), 2013

Inexplicably, in the late 1950s, the drugstore owned by Jim Hawkins, at the south end of Boonville, had a large sign hanging outside stating "Booneville Drugs," clearly shown in a postcard entitled "Booneville, Calif." (15d). In both instances, there is middle "e" in Booneville. See "Discovery of Anderson Valley," plus #25 and #28, for further discussion of the mysterious middle "e"…

15d. Booneville(?) Business District, circa Late 1950s

16. THE LIVE OAK BUILDING (1926-PRESENT)
On the right—in the "heart" of SoBo, opposite Fairground Offices

The original Live Oak Garage (see #11) had been a great success, but being on the outskirts of town meant it was not realizing its full potential. As a result, in 1926, CAT and his wife Marie purchased a piece of ground closer to town and constructed a new building in the heart of the business district (16a). This served as a repair and machine shop as well as having new gas pumps installed, along with an oil storage room and other necessary items to be a full service station. The building was located directly across from the Mendocino County Fair building and it kept its name "The Live Oak Garage" (16c). As can be seen in the photograph it was in the heart of the business district, with several stores and businesses in close proximity.

After CAT passed away in 1946, Glenn McAbee, who had worked for CAT all of these years, took over and ran the business for CAT's wife, Marie. Around this time, Glenn's son, Richard (Dick), got out of the service after World War II and went to work as a mechanic with his father. In 1962, Dick quit the garage and went to work with the California Division of Forestry as a mechanic. After Glenn passed away in 1965, CAT's wife Marie closed the shop, and sometime later she sold the place. It was initially converted into a private school but for many, many years it operated as a church building, although recently it was bought by a winery and is rumored to be the future location of various retail outlets. We shall see, but whatever it may be, let's hope that the new owners respect history and leave this grand old building with the name "The Live Oak Building" (16b & 16d).

(It should be noted that the unique logo on the building's front was added by those two buddies and "partners-in-crime, and obviously art," Wayne Ahrens and Tom English.)

P.S. The unusually shaped hill, with tentacle-like ridges on every side, about a mile north of Boonville on the east side of Hwy 128, is Tarwater Hill, named after CAT. Old-timers will not hear of it being referred to as "Octopus Hill"—a name that arose following the "hippy invasion" of the late sixties and seventies, for reasons somewhat understandable if you stare at it long enough!

16a. Live Oak building and downtown, 1928

16b. Live Oak Building and downtown, 2013

16c. Live Oak Building, 1932

16d. Live Oak Building, 2013

17. THE COUNTY FAIRGROUNDS
On the left—opposite the Live Oak Building

In 1926 John T. Farrer, Fred Rawles, Herman Alberts, and Tom Ruddock attended the Cloverdale Citrus Fair and afterwards, with the encouragement and support of Cecil Gowan, they called together a group of local people and discussed the possibility of having an apple show in Boonville. This idea was well accepted by all and the first Apple Show in Anderson Valley was held in October 1927 (17a). Prior to that, there had been an Apple Show in the town of Mendocino since the early 1900s.

This was a great success and continued in this form until 1937 when Judge Harwood June, who was the Director of the Apple Show, traveled to Sacramento with Fred Rawles and Tom Ruddock, this time joined by Chester Estell, to talk with legislators to gain permission to list the fair as the "Mendocino County Fair and Apple Show." Permission was granted and the first fair building was constructed with donated money, lumber, hardware, and labor, and the first fair with its new name was held in October, 1938 (17b). That first fair was built on an acre-and-a-half of land, whereas today it encompasses 35 acres. Just like today, however, the Apple Hall saw many dances and social events. In 1958, a new complex was built with many new and modern features.

In more recent years a new and larger hall was built, along with a new office, dining hall, and kitchen, plus a new front on the building (17c). The complex is located directly across the street from the Live Oak Building in the middle of town, and remains a place used by Valley folks for many social events and gatherings, as well as the County Fair, of course.

17a. First Apple Show, Boonville 1927

17b. First County Fair, Boonville 1938

17c. County Fairgrounds, Boonville 2014

18. RICHMOND STORE / ANDERSON VALLEY MARKET

On the right—just past Lauren's Restaurant

Two brothers by the name of Harry and Walter Richmond bought a building in the early 1930s in the mid-part of town and started a grocery store. This store was rather unique for the time in that the brothers extended a roof out over a forecourt in front of the store and installed two gas pumps. As a result local folks could buy their groceries and gas up their automobile with one stop—not a common thing back then (18a).

Later, Harry (pictured above) bought out Walter and ran the store until the late 1940s, when he sold it to the Huff family, who then sold on to a Mr. Roy Elliot. By this time there were other gas stations in town so Elliot decided to have the gas pumps removed from in front of the store and took down the lean-to roof.

In the mid-1960s, Elliot sold the store to Clarence Galletti and his wife Rena, along with their business partners Frank Falleri and his wife, Leonore. The two couples also owned the grocery store just north of downtown Philo, previously owned by George and Betty Burns. They ran both stores until the one in Philo burned down and later became the Starr Auto repair shop that is there today. (The office building that is alongside Starr Auto was once The Style Shop and was run by Charmian Blattner, sister of Betty Burns.) They carried out some major remodeling of the store in Boonville with a complete metal building constructed over the outside of the old building which was then torn down from the inside.

After a few years, in around 1970, Galletti sold the store to Mr. Rubin Thomasson, Sr. and his wife Marie. Rubin Sr. constructed an addition on to the back of the store, and a few years later in 1978 the store was turned over to their son Rubin Jr. and his wife, Beryl, who continue to own and operate the popular store today (18b).

18a. Richmond Store, 1930s

18b. Anderson Valley Market, 2013

19. FINNEY / FERRELL / ROSSI HARDWARE
On the left—Rossi Hardware. Opposite the A.V. Market

Around 1890, C. W. (Charley) Finney, better known as "Dime" Finney, became the fourth owner of this hardware and sporting goods store in the center of town. He was nicknamed "Dime" because he priced everything in the store to even dollars plus a dime. Charley also opened a machine shop on the north side of the store (19a), where he provided his great skills at repairing guns.

In 1918, a man named Albert Ferrell bought the Finney store. In about 1930 he tore it down and built a new hardware store, adding a full-service gasoline station beside the store to the south side a year later (19c). Just to the south of the station and next to the Apple Fair Building he built a house for his family to live in. Being in the hardware business, Albert was given the nickname "Paint Brush."

In 1945, Ferrell sold the store and business to a Mr. John Rossi who had moved out here from New York. John ran and operated the store until the late 1950s or early 1960s when he retired and turned the store over to his son, Emil Rossi. Emil ran the store and improved the stock until about 2010 when he "kind of" retired and turned the business over to his two sons, Chris and Nick Rossi. It remains one of only two hardware stores in the entire Valley. From the photographs you can see how little the building has changed since the early 1930s (19b & 19d).

19a. Finney's Store, 1915

19b. Rossi Hardware, 2012

19c. Ferrell Store, 1932

19d. Rossi Hardware, 2012

20. The Boonville Lodge
On the right—past the A.V. Market
(Currently under the sign "Boonville Saloon")

Shortly after the end of prohibition in 1933, this building sprang up and became very well known as the town's main "hornin' region" (which is translated as "bar" in the local Boontling dialect). Local folklore has it that many men have spilled their blood fighting their way out of this bar and thus its nickname "The Bucket of Blood."

It is unknown who the original builder and owners of the bar were, although by the mid-1930s the owners were Mr. Russell Tolman and his wife, Helen (20a). Russell and Helen separated, and it was agreed that Helen would keep the bar. She owned and operated the business until the mid-1940s, at some point getting married to a Mr. Lackey. They added a small room onto the side of the bar and opened up a restaurant. They also added some small cabins to the back of the bar and rented them out to local people.

In 1945, the bar was bought by A.O. Stornetta, a dairy farmer from Point Arena, who passed it on to his son-in-law and daughter, Russell and Gladys Mann, and their business partners—Rena Falleri and her husband Clarence Galletti. The two couples ran the business for about five years until 1950 when the Gallettis sold their half to the Manns and opened a general store in Philo with his partner Frank Falleri. (They later also took over at the Anderson Valley Market in Boonville—see #18.)

The Manns continued to run the bar but eventually the old building was torn down and was replaced by a new one that housed a new version of The Boonville Lodge. In the mid-1960s, Russell and Gladys carried out further remodeling to the building, expanding it on the south side to increase the size of the restaurant, and added a redwood exterior on the front.

In 1973, the Manns, after almost thirty years of ownership, sold the business to Tom Verdon and his wife, Rosetta, who made some changes and renovations, including expanding the restaurant and replacing the redwood front with brick. Since that time, there have been many changes in ownership, including folks such as Ron Jones, for a short time; then Joaquin Pacheco, who owned the bar for about 15 years and who opened up the general store and Laundromat next door; Urs and Dolores Schaub; John and Candy Green with Bobby and Shelly Mayberry; Tom Towey and Carroll Pratt; and most recently, Marcia Martinez and Shelly Mayberry, again, who operated under the name "The Boonville Saloon" before closing down in late 2013. At the time of writing, the bar and the restaurant space next door remain closed but a general store on the bar's other side called "Pick and Pay" remains open and would appear to be a thriving business (20b).

20a. Boonville Lodge, circa 1934

20b. Pick and Pay Grocery / Boonville Lodge, 2013

21. THE MISSOURI HOUSE
On the left—just past the Post Office

Sometime in the 1870s this large single-story building was constructed and was initially owned by Mr. W.K. Dillingham. In July of 1884, the house was sold to Mr. T.J. (Jeff) and Martha Vestal for $500. It was named The Missouri House shortly thereafter. In 1905, another name was added, "The Anderson Valley Hotel," and the Vestals ran this business for many years. It was particularly noted for its well water that provided the guests with a very cool, palatable product. (21a).

In later years, after the hotel closed in 1939, the house was converted into a family home and was owned by Harwood and Blossom June (daughter of Jeff Vestal). Harwood eventually became the first Justice of the Peace in Boonville, and he opened a courtroom right there in the house.

In more recent times the house has undergone some major renovations and now has offices inside for local small businesses, although it still stands in the same location as it always has—just north of the present post office. It remains a very attractive building that maintains its original look in many ways, although a recent change has been the name change to the "K Howland Gallery" (21b).

21a. The Missouri House, 1915

21b. The Missouri House, 2012

22. J. T. Farrer Building and Store
Two-story structure on the right in central Boonville

Back in the mid-1880s this building was constructed to house a general merchandise store. It is believed to have been built by George Tansy Brown, the carpenter son of Doc Brown. George was the first owner of the store too, and the Valley's first telephone was situated here. George lived in the house behind the building, where all five of his daughters were born.

In the early 1900s, after a number of different owners had operated the business, Mr. John T. Farrer and his wife, Florence, bought it and began what would be a long and significant contribution to the community (22a). They added and changed merchandise many times in order to supply local folks with the necessary items to fit the people's changing needs over the years.

In order to accommodate everyone, Mrs. Farrer had a room in the bottom of the store built just for ladies apparel. This was the only place in the Valley that handled these items—the Valley's first lingerie store!

The building has two stories and upstairs there is a very large room that was used for a dance hall in the early years of the 20th century. However, by the mid-1920s it was noticed that during dances the building began to sway back and forth and the dances were discontinued. In the later years of the Farrers time at the building, the upstairs was used as a movie theater.

Sometime in the early 1920s, Mr. Farrer built a gas station next to the store—where the Anytime Saloon (#23) had previously stood. Part of this building still stands in the same place today—as the Paysanne ice cream parlor.

By the mid-1950s the Farrers decided to retire but they kept the store inventory. That way, even though it was closed, if someone needed something, then Mr. Farrer would open up and get whatever the person wanted.

Following the passing of the Farrers, nobody wanted to continue the business so the building was sold to a firm from Ukiah—Parducci Winery, in around 1979. They had it for several years and it was given a major remodeling both inside and out before being sold to Ken Allen in 1987, who at the same time bought the property next door, the lot where Wiese's Valley Inn had stood before burning down, and turned that into the Buckhorn brew pub.

Allen kept the Farrer Building, with its various small business tenants, for almost twenty years before it was purchased by local hotelier / chef John Schmitt and his business partners in 2006. It now houses three small businesses on the ground floor, plus the ice cream store, and is the office for several more upstairs, including the Anderson Valley Advertiser newspaper. It is still a remarkable-looking building (22b) as well as being one of the classic old-time Valley landmarks.

22a. The J. T. Farrer Building, circa 1900

22b. The J. T. Farrer Building, 2013

23. THE ANYTIME SALOON

On the right—small building at the north end of the Farrer Building

The Anytime Saloon was originally located on the northwest side of the J.T. Farrer store in the heart of Boonville, being built sometime around the late-1880s. It was owned and run by Jim Watson and named The Anytime because a person could go there and get an alcoholic drink any time they desired (23a).

In 1903, the women of the town, annoyed by the excessive drinking by the menfolk, banded together and voted for a local dry region, preventing the sale of alcohol within the town. This caused the saloon business to fold. The owner of The Anytime, Emitt Mc-Gimsey, decided to move the building outside the town limits. He moved it to the vicinity of the current gravel pits, near to the junction of "Poor Way" (now Highway 253) and Highway 128, where it was renamed The Anyhow—a place where, despite local prohibition, you could go and have a drink "anyhow" for it was outside of the town proper and therefore beyond the jurisdiction of that law.

A few years later, another local election was held and the earlier "prohibition" was repealed. This resulted in other options for folks to buy alcohol in Boonville opening up, which severely slowed down the saloon business out there on the edge of town. Not long after this The Anyhow was closed and stood vacant for some years until folks by the name of Slim and Nina Vallier bought the building. They moved it back into town, to a location across the street from the Boonville Lodge, next to The Missouri House (#21) in Boonville. There it was remodeled and converted into a restaurant by the name of "Ye Olde Hayloft Inn."

From the 1930s, the spot alongside the Farrer Building where the Anytime Saloon had stood, was occupied for many years by a small gas station (Farrer's—see Buckhorn 27e). Today, this is the location of the Paysanne ice cream store, with the gas pump still in front (23b).

23a. The Anytime Saloon, circa 1890

23b. Paysanne ice cream, 2013

THE ANYTIME SALOON (CONT.)

Meanwhile, Ye Olde Hayloft Inn did not do very well as a restaurant and soon closed, remaining so until sometime in the mid-1940s when it was moved once again—all the way to its present site, several miles north, in the heart of Philo! It became a restaurant and has since changed ownership and names several times, one of which was Janie's Place (owned by Janie Morse). It is presently owned and operated as Libby's, a very popular restaurant in the Valley serving Cal Mex food (23c).

23c. Libby's Restaurant in Philo, 2014

24. THE LAMBERT HOUSE
Left off Hwy 128, opposite The Buckhorn, down Lambert Lane,
½ mile on the left before the bridge

In the early years of the century, the Lambert family, shown here in 1906, lived in this old house (24a—date of construction unknown), and gave their family name to the narrow road, constructed in around 1904, that leads there from Highway 128 alongside the Boonville Hotel's parking lot.

The house and property has changed hands several times and was once the home of Vernon and Martha Rawles and their family. After Vernon's passing, Martha moved into an apartment, and her son Bob Rawles lived there until around the early 1960s when Gene and Berna Walker bought the house and property.

The Walkers have lived in the house ever since, and raised a family of five children there. Gene and Berna have done some remodeling of the house and it remains a beautiful old two-story house today (24b).

24a. Lambert House (Lambert Lane), circa 1906

24b. Walker House (Lambert Lane), 2012

25. DOWNTOWN BOONVILLE LOOKING NORTH

Photographs taken from middle of the road, fifty feet south of the Farrer Building

The town had been named after the man that built the hotel—Alonzo Kendall, which he opened in 1864. The building was the first significant building in this particular area at the time. Prior to this, the main town was located on the corner of the Ukiah road and McDonald's-to-the-Sea Road, or what today is the corner of Highway 128 and Highway 253, and for a time was called, appropriately, The Corners. After Mr. Kendall completed building the hotel, some of the businesses moved to this area from the Corners and soon a small town started to develop. It was then decided to name the settlement Kendall City.

Mr. Kendall ran the hotel for a few years before his health deteriorated, and in 1867 he decided to return to the Manchester area on the coast from where he had originally come. At some point around 1857-58, the Boone family arrived in town, led by William Waightstall Boone. Mr. Boone purchased a store from Mr. Levi Straus, who had moved on to bigger things, and became the postmaster. It is also thought that Mr. Boone ran the hotel at some point following Mr. Kendall's departure for the coast in 1867. Around that time the local people decided to change the name of this settlement from Kendall City to its new name of Boonville, after the aforementioned W.W. Boone, who lived in Anderson Valley until 1870, when he and his family moved back to Missouri, where Boone died in 1876.

(Author's note—An explanation for the name being Boonville without an "e" in the middle is given earlier in the book in "Discovery of Anderson Valley," but formal Valley resident and keen amateur historian, Jodie Bucshman, has a different explanation. She states, "This can be explained in that the Great Register of Mendocino County has the name typed as 'Boon, William Waitsell,' (the spelling of the middle name is also incorrect) dated: June 23, 1866. Add to that the 1870 Census lists the family as 'Boon, William W,' dated: August 2, 1870. My guess is that the 1870 Census simply followed the typed error on the 1866 Great Register. The Boone family must have departed in very close time proximity to the 1870 Census to enable them to arrive back in Hickory County, Missouri, where their eighth child was born in May of 1871." See also #15 and #28.) .

This first photograph (25a) depicts a gathering of the local people, 40-plus in all (probably the total population at that time), that is believed to have been taken at the celebration on the day the name of the town changed in the late 1860s. The building on the extreme right was the store that Mr. Boone ran, and the big white building on the left was the hotel, with some people on the balcony. The house on the extreme left was the home of the W.W. Boone family and also the post office. Taking a closer look, one can see Mr. Boone, his wife, and two children standing at the corner of their house.

Today (25b) that same view shows the Farrer Building (#22) on the right with the old gas pump outside the ice cream shop (#23). Trees hide The Buckhorn (#27) but the General Store can be seen clearly, as can Aquarelle Restaurant with the blue roof. On the left side of the highway is the red-painted Boonville Hotel and its parking lot—formerly the site of the post office and Boone's house. Lambert Lane can also be seen—a road that came into being around 1904.

25a. Boonville (looking north), circa 1867

25b. Boonville (looking north), 2013

26. DOWNTOWN BOONVILLE LOOKING SOUTH

Photographs taken from middle of the road, outside the Boonville Hotel

This photograph (26a), dated specifically as October 23rd, 1909, shows what was probably a regular street scene of the time. On the far left is the Whipple Meat Market, later St. John's, Wiese's Restaurant, and The Buckhorn pub, while further down the street is the Farrer Building with its porch that remains to this day. The building in between is where The Anytime Saloon had been situated. The bar had been moved to the southern outskirts of the town following a local prohibition ordinance. In its place is the forerunner of what was to become Farrer's gas station.

On the right in the distance is the Finney Hardware Store and machine shop—later Rossi's Hardware, and in the foreground the larger building on the right is Antrum's Store, with the smaller structure believed to be the post office in what would later become the hotel parking lot—see photograph 28c.

The recent photograph (26b) looking south at the town features, on the east side of the road, The Buckhorn, the Farrer Building, the Pick and Pay store, the A.V. Market, and in the far distance Lauren's Restaurant and the Live Oak Building. On the right side of the street is Rossi's, and the post office can be made out through the trees, along with the Missouri House (#21) and the two-story Tolman House. In the right foreground are Lambert Lane and the Boonville Hotel parking lot.

26a. Boonville (looking south), 1909

26b. Boonville (looking south), 2012

27. ST. JOHN'S / WIESE'S VALLEY INN / THE BUCKHORN

On the right (The Buckhorn)—opposite Lambert Lane

Around 1930, the building that had previously housed McGimsey's Meat Market as early as 1909 (see #26a—far left) was remodeled by the new owners, Sadie and Bill St. John, and converted into a restaurant, grocery store, and ice cream shop (27a). Over time, a barber shop and a shoe repair shop were also added inside the store.

In 1940, Ernest and Marie Wiese purchased the store, and soon afterwards Ernest added a room onto the south side of the original building and turned it into a bar (27b). In the 1940s and 1950s the restaurant and fountain shop served a range of folks in the Valley and was regarded as a great place for the teenagers to hang out. In 1954, the Wieses remodeled the place, complete with a modern-looking front to the store (27c). The same view today (27d) is of a fine-looking building that is a popular destination for local residents and tourists alike.

Photographs 27e, 27f, and 27g show this building from the north side. It was clearly part of a thriving downtown business community in the 1930s, with Farrer's gas station open next door and Tindall's Meat Market and The Boonville Lodge further down the street (27e). By the 1940s, it was also a bus stop for the Hackley Stage Coach Company (27f).

Wiese's Bar was one of three bars operating in town during the timber and sawmill boom days—along with The Track Inn (#14) and The Boonville Lodge (#20). There were no banks in Anderson Valley so Ernest Wiese would go to Cloverdale just a day or two before payday at the mills and bring back huge amounts of cash so that the workers could cash their paychecks. Obviously this made for excellent bar business.

On April 1st, 1963, there was a fierce fire and the building burned to the ground. Wiese never rebuilt the store and the lot stood empty for many years before it was sold to a Mr. Strange, who kept it briefly before selling it to Ken Allen. Mr. Allen cleaned the lot and, together with David Norfleet, constructed a new large building. In 1987, this opened as the Anderson Valley Brewery with its own bar and restaurant and the name "The Buckhorn Saloon"—named after a bar that had operated in the Valley back in the 1870s.

Allen opened his new brewery at the south end of town in the late 1990s and sold the bar business to Diana Charles but remained the landlord. Diana (see #41) was a popular bar owner and did well for a time, but eventually the business could not cover the overhead and she closed. The business was reopened by Jason Schreider as "The Highpockety Ox" (Boontling for "pompous ass," approximately) that survived for a couple of years, but unfortunately for Schreider he had signed an onerous rental agreement, and in February 2008 "The Ox" could no longer meet the expenses and it too had to close.

The building remained empty for a couple of years until 2010 when the property was sold to Gary and Ginny Island. In March of 2011, Tom Towey, who with Carroll Pratt had previously owned The Boonville Lodge, opened "The Buckhorn, Boonville," a restaurant / bar that is the only "gastro pub" in the Valley, with a large selection of draft beers, wines, cocktails, and pub grub (27g).

27a. St John's store, 1930s

27b. Wiese's Valley Inn, Early 1940s

27c. Wiese's Valley Inn, Early 1950s

27d. The Buckhorn, 2014

27e. St. John's / Farrer Building, 1930s

27f. Wiese's Valley Inn, Late 1940s

27g. The Buckhorn, 2013

28. JOE ANTRUM'S STORE / POST OFFICE / BOONVILLE HOTEL PARKING LOT

On the left—Boonville Hotel parking lot

Shortly before the turn of the century, this large two-story building was constructed on the north corner of Highway 128 and what came to be by 1904 Lambert Lane. It was Joe Antrum's Dry Goods store. On the ground floor, along with dry goods, it also stocked grocery items as well as farm supplies, while the large room upstairs was used as a dance hall.

A short distance from the front corner of the building a flagpole was installed that was about 60 feet tall (28a). The old-timers used to say that when a man went into the "Bucket of Blood" bar (The Boonville Lodge—#20) and had several drinks too many, he would come out higher than Dwight's Flag Pole. In the background of this photograph, taken around 1900, you can clearly see The Boonville Hotel. Also, on the right, you can spot part of the sign for The Anytime Saloon (moved to the outskirts of town in 1903—see #23), alongside the Cash Store that was a part of the Farrer Building.

(Author's Note—In this circa 1900 photograph the word "Boonville" on the "Cash Store" sign has no "e" in the middle. Some folks believe it was originally "Booneville" and that the "e" in the middle of the name was dropped at some point between the early-1870s, by which time W.W. Boone (after whom the town was named) had moved away, and the mid-1880s when "Boonville" appears in official documents. We believe at this point, like most other folks, that there never was a middle "e"—see "Discovery of Anderson Valley - Authors Notes" for a full explanation, or #25 for an alternative point of view—but the debate continues, and photographs like the one earlier in the book (15d), certainly confused us for a time…)

Around 1920, Joe Antrum sold the store to a Mr. Sam McAbee who ran it for a short time. Antrum and McAbee had a disagreement about payments on the store purchase and soon after a fire broke out that completely burned the building down. Some folks believe this was very suspicious.

In the late 1920s there were two smaller buildings constructed on the lot—one was a feed store owned by Lester Bivans; the other, a post office (28c), with Mr. Lawson as postmaster, situated on virtually the same spot where Boonville's first post office had stood when operated by W.W. Boone in the late 1860s—see 25a. Eventually these buildings were torn down—the post office moving to what was, by the 1940s, Tindall's Market (see 15b). Today the space serves as the parking lot for the Boonville Hotel as well as the Saturday morning home of the Boonville Farmers Market throughout the summer (28b & 28d).

28a. Antrum's Store from Farrer Building, circa 1900

28b. Hotel parking lot from Farrer Building, 2014

28c. Boonville Post Office, 1920s

28d. Hotel parking lot, 2012

29. THE BOONVILLE HOTEL
On the left in central Boonville

In 1864, Mr. Alonso Kendall built a hotel that at that time was the only large building in the area (shown in 1905—29a). Up until that point in time, the main town of Boonville, which was called The Corners, had been located at the junction of Highway 128 and the Ukiah Road (later Highway 253). Upon completion of his hotel, Mr. Kendall modestly decided to rename the surrounding settlement Kendall City!

A short time later, Mr. W. W. Boone arrived in the area and soon became the postmaster, eventually leading to a change in the town's name to Boonville in the late-1860s following Kendall's departure to the coast for health reasons. The hotel remained in the same location until, in the 1920s, it had to be moved back about 30 feet in order to make way for the new highway that was being built through the heart of town. (29c—before the hotel was moved back).

During the lifespan of the building there have been some 20 different owners of the Hotel and it has undergone some major remodeling over the years. Some of those owners were the likes of McAbee, Stepp, Bostwick, Landerbee, Hayes, Peck, Christensen, Rickard, McGimsey, Duff, Sanders, Handley, Berry, Nielson*, Cronquist, Carsey, the unforgettable Vern and Charlene Rollins and, since 1988, Johnny Schmitt and his business partners. Today it has a restaurant as well as the several rooms and a couple of cabins, all of which generally cater to Valley visitors. Over each summer the venue plays host to several weddings (29b & 29d).

* In the 1950s, Newt Nielson owned the Hotel and also had a number of German shepherd dogs that he dearly loved. He had determined that they would all take part in the annual County Fair Parade one day and arranged for that to happen at a fair in the late-1950s, However, just days before the event, one of his dogs passed away. True to his word, Nielson marched along the highway in the parade with all of his dogs, including the one who had just died, in a wheelbarrow being pushed by the proud owner!

Footnote: Bill Kimberlin, a local history buff of some repute, comments: "The Boonville Hotel is mentioned in Jack London's wife's diary, which is in the San Francisco Historical Society. The diary mentions that Jack was commissioned by a New York newspaper to cover the San Francisco Earthquake in 1906. After that article, he went to Santa Rosa to file a story and then to the Mendocino Coast.

"The diary states that they returned via Anderson Valley, stopping in Philo for lunch and staying at "Mrs. Berry's place" in Boonville. The Berrys owned the Boonville Hotel at the time and London famously signed the hotel register.

"I always wondered what his mode of transportation was. Finally, Norm Clow told me that his mother or aunt or some family member encountered the Londons on horseback, somewhere in the Valley."

Current owner Johnny Schmitt reports that, according to an old guest register, the infamous Jesse James also stayed at the Hotel in its early days.

29a. Boonville Hotel, 1905

29b. Boonville Hotel, 2014

29c. Boonville Hotel, 1914

29d. Boonville Hotel, 2013

30. THE CLAUDE PRESLEY HOUSE

On the right—opposite the Redwood Drive-In
(At the start of Mrs. Harris Lane)

It has been difficult to acquire much history on this old house, although it is believed to have been built somewhere around the turn of the century and some folks believe it is the oldest family home still standing in central Boonville. One thing that is known about its early years is that the Bert and Pearl Paul family along with their children lived in the house in the late 1920s and early 1930s (30a). By the mid-30s they moved on to a bigger house to accommodate their growing number of children and the Dightman family moved in to this property and lived there up until the late 1930's. Following the Dightmans, Maurice and Alice Tindall moved in with their daughter Marilyn. All during this time, and up until the late 1940s or early 1950s, the property was owned by Mr. Claude Presley.

In the early 1970s, the house and the store next door were sold by Elsie Skerbeck to Dale Hulbert, and the flowers for Dale's flower and nursery store were grown behind the buildings. Hulbert then sold it to realtors Bob Mathias and Don Starks in 1979.

Today (30b), the house and the Boont Berry Farm health food and deli store next door are owned by Burt Cohen, and the house appears to have remained pretty much as it has over many years. It is located directly across the road from the Redwood Drive-In, next door to the Boont Berry Store.

Debate continues about what is the Oldest Family Home in Boonville. Some folks think it is this one—the Presley House. Others say it is the Duff / Grandma June House (#31) or the Prather / Rose Place (#32). However, with both Grandma June's and Prather's on the outskirts of the town, there is no doubt which is the oldest "downtown" Boonville family home—the Claude Presley House.

30a. Claude Presley House, circa 1930s

30b. Central Boonville's oldest family home(?), 2013

31. THE DUFF / GRANDMA JUNE HOUSE / CENTER PROPERTY

On the left of Hwy 128, on the north side of the junction of Hwy 128
and Mountain View Road

This house (31a) was built sometime in the 1880s and is one of the oldest family homes in Boonville★. However, it is not known who built it or who lived in it until sometime before 1900 when Delilah Duff and her family lived there. There are actually two houses on the property, and the other one, known as the Grandma June House (31c), is almost as old and was where the Duffs started making caskets. They did so until late 1922 when widow Duff sold the place to a Doctor Levi J. Tabler. The doctor converted the house into a hospital, and this was the only place in the Valley that was capable of performing such services as surgery, mending broken bones, and delivering babies.

In October, 1928, Dr. Tabler and his wife Mary J. Tabler sold the houses and property to Mrs. Severena June—shown on the porch in photograph 31a, who had been recently widowed following the death of husband, John June.

Many years later, in her will written in 1948, Severena left the property to what some family members regarded as a church cult, for the grand sum of "Love and affection and $10." Other family members strongly believed Grandma June had made a considered decision and was in sound mind. She died in 1949 and the church folks owned the property for a short time before Severena's son, Harwood J. June, was able to buy it from them after he truthfully told them that many of the furnishings, etc. were his mother's and that he had sentimental value attached to them.

When Harwood passed away in 1967 he left the property to his wife Blossom who, when she died in 1991, left it to their three children, Evelyn, Delmar, and Jack. They went on to separate the June properties, with Evelyn getting the Missouri House (#21), Jack receiving the post office building (the current one), and Delmer inheriting Grandma June's property.

Following Delmar's passing, he left the property to his daughter, Victoria Center, a current member of the Board of Directors for the Anderson Valley Museum and Historical Society, so that today the old houses and property still remain in the hands of a member of the June family (31c and 31d).

★ The debate continues as to which is the oldest family home still standing in Boonville. It would appear that it is one of the following: this Duff House; the Presley House (#30); or the Prather / Rose Place (#32)—to be further debated…

31a. Duff / Grandma June Place, circa Late 1930s

31b. June / Center Property, 2014

31c. Grandma June House, circa 1960s

31d. June / Center Property, 2013

ANDERSON VALLEY WAY

(Left at 28.02 mile-marker on Hwy 128)

32. THE ROSE / SAM PRATHER HOUSE

Anderson Valley Way★—at the 28.02 mile marker turn left off Hwy 128.
1st house on the right

The photo here (32a) shows the old William J. Rose house in approximately 1888 with members of the Rose family and a team of horses and the stagecoach out front. Among his many jobs, and while also maintaining the little ranch, William Rose was the stagecoach driver for several years. He drove the stage from Cloverdale to Boonville and then from Boonville on to Albion over on the coast.

William's daughter, Martha Rose, inherited the house when her father passed. She married Frank Guntly, although it was still referred to as the Rose Place. The family moved out in the 1940s, and it was rented to Pat Hulbert's family. In the mid-1940s, Martha and Frank sold the place to a Mr. Roland Kingwell and his family, who were cousins to the Rose family.

In the late-1940s, Mr. Kingwell took a job driving the school bus for the Anderson Valley School District, a career that continued until 1966 when he retired and moved, selling the house and acreage around it to Albert (Sam) Prather.

Since that time Sam has built a barn on the property as well as a two-car garage, and in the early 2000s he remodeled inside and out. Sam is one of the Valley's finest sheep ranchers, with several locations on which he keeps his flocks. Shepherds like him are in short supply these days, and he continues to raise and breed registered sheep that have won many prizes at the County Fair over the years.

This well-maintained house (32b) is seen as a credit to the community after standing for nearly 120 years.★★

★ This is known as A.V. Way entrance #1. The other A.V. Way entrances, #2 and #3, are at mile markers 26.94 and 25.45 respectively off Hwy 128.

★★ The debate continues as to which is the oldest family home still standing in Boonville. It would appear that it is one of the following: this Prather / Rose Place; the Presley House (#30); or the Grandma June property (#31).

32a. The Rose House, circa 1880s

32b. The Prather House, 2012

33. THE FRY / WASSON-SMITH HOUSE

Anderson Valley Way—½ mile north from the south entrance to Anderson Valley Way;
on the left, 100' past the driveway to St. Elizabeth Seton Catholic
Church Refectory on the other side

This house was built sometime in the late 1890s (33a), along with a considerable amount of arable, flat-bottomed land. As time passed, the Fry family struggled to maintain the land and buildings and the taxes began to build up to the point where it became necessary to sell the property. In 1931, Harwood June raised enough money to acquire the ranch and house for the price of the taxes.

Harwood worked on improving the place by planting apple orchards along with alfalfa hay fields and also a very large, modern apple-packing shed. His son, Delmar June, built a motel between the house and the packing shed, which today is the apartment complex known as "Tijuanita" in the local Mexican community. Delmar also did some remodeling on the old house so that he and his wife Barbara could live there. Later Delmar purchased a piece of land just south of this location and built a house of his own at which point the June family rented the old house to various people for several years.

After Harwood and his wife Blossom passed on, his daughter Evelyn Berry was named as administrator of the estate. In 1975, a rancher from the Russian River Valley, near Healdsburg, by the name of Phillip Wasson, purchased many properties and buildings on the west side of Anderson Valley Way, including the old Fry house. Wasson kept the house rented until 1986, when his daughter Jan and her husband Robert Smith moved in.

Jan and Robert have made this their home now for the past 28 years. This old house is still of very strong structure and has had some remodeling done to it (33b) over the years, with the result that it has been lived in by a various Valley folks continually for nearly 120 years.

33a. The Fry House, circa 1890s

33b. Wasson–Smith House, 2014

34. OLD ANDERSON VALLEY HIGH SCHOOLS
Anderson Valley Way, on the left, opposite A.V. Museum

The first Anderson Valley High School was started in the fall of 1912 (34a). It was a one-room building between two large barns close to where the current elementary school stands (34b). It had one principal / teacher who instructed all students, with a four-year curriculum. Each year another room was added to the building until there were five rooms.

The other school in the area was a one-room school called Con Creek elementary school—what became known as the Little Red Schoolhouse as both a school and later the Valley's Museum.

In 1924, a new school was constructed just 100 feet to the south on the same property (34c). This was a large multi-room school with a gymnasium and a stage for plays, and was the education center for many of Valley children for many years. In 1958, a new school facility was constructed and opened about a mile and a half south of the old school, on Mountain View Road just north of the center of Boonville. The reason given for the move was that the foundation at the older school was gone. Pat Hulbert, who graduated from the above school, recalls, "When they tore the building down they had to dynamite the foundation—what does that say about the reason?"

Today the site of that old high school is where the present school district's administration offices are located (34d).

34a. Anderson Valley High School, circa 1916

34b. Anderson Valley Elementary School, 2014

34c. Anderson Valley High School, 1924

34d. Anderson Valley Schools' District Office, 2012

35. THE LITTLE WHITE - RED SCHOOLHOUSE / ANDERSON VALLEY MUSEUM

Anderson Valley Way, on the right opposite the Elementary School
At #2 entrance to Anderson Valley Way

In 1891, on land donated specifically for a new school by William Wallach, Sr., (see #10), the Con Creek School was opened and the children had a new schoolhouse. The first teacher in this new schoolhouse was a Mrs. Annie McGimsey. At that time the schoolhouse faced the west and was on the east side of the highway—which we now know as Anderson Valley Way. Over the years changes were made to the building that included a long front porch being added after the 1906 earthquake (35a). Then, in 1940, a back room was added to serve as a library.

When the rights of way were purchased in order to build an expressway through the Valley it was necessary to move the building a short distance to the north. It also resulted in the building being turned ¼ turn in a clockwise direction to face the northwest.

From 1941 to 1958 the school was used for the 7th and 8th grades only. Following the construction of the elementary school across the road on Anderson Valley Way in the mid-1950s and the opening of the new high school in town in 1958 (see #34), the Con Creek School was used as a kindergarten school. In November 1963, the old white school was painted red and was dedicated as the "Little Red Schoolhouse," which it remained until 1979 when it was closed permanently as a school. Therefore, officially, it was actually only a "Little Red Schoolhouse" for sixteen years.

At that time, the Anderson Valley Community Services District purchased the school and property and leased it to the Anderson Valley Historical Society for a museum. In October, 1979 it was placed on the National Register of Historical Landmarks. After standing on this location for over 120 years it now remains as the Anderson Valley Museum and houses many fascinating items from Anderson Valley's storied history—a place we strongly urge you to visit and support. After all, it's not known as "The Best Little Museum in the West" without reason! (35b)

35a. Con Creek School House, Late 1930s

35b. Anderson Valley Museum, 2013

HIGHWAY 128

36. THE TOM RUDDOCK HOUSE

Hwy 128: 600' past the 23.75 mile marker
Left on Ruddock Rd South, just past Golden Eye Winery
On the right, behind The Madrones buildings

The original Ruddock home was located on the south side of Indian Creek and about one quarter of a mile upstream from the highway. It is unknown how long the family lived in this location before, in 1934, Tom Ruddock constructed a large two-story house where he and his wife raised three children, shown in the photograph—twins Tom and Jerry, with little Mary (36a).

Tom was known throughout the valley by the nickname of "Pine Limb." It is believed that he came by this name because he was regarded as "tougher than a pine limb," although some old-timers believe it was because at some point he hit someone over the head with a pine limb!

Tom was a hard-working rancher as well as a very prominent figure throughout the Valley. In 1927, he and three other local gentlemen, John Farrer, Herman Alberts, and Fred Rawles, got together and started the very first Apple Show in Boonville (see #17). Later, in 1937, Ruddock and Rawles were joined by Judge Harwood June and Chester Estell when they went to Sacramento to meet with legislators to get the event listed as the "Mendocino County Fair and Apple Show," which was to open the following year.

After Tom and his wife passed away, their daughter and her husband remained living in the old house. Now that those two have also passed on, Tom's granddaughter and grandson live in the house. Thus the old house has served as a home for three generations of the Ruddock family (36b).

36a. Tom Ruddock's, 1934

36b. Ruddock family home, 2012

PHILO–DOWNTOWN

37. SCHOOLS IN PHILO /
BAXTER WINERY TASTING ROOM /
PG&E SUBSTATION

Hwy 128: 23.00 mile marker in Philo—on left (38a & b)
And down Philo School Road on right off Hwy 128,
on the corner at the left-hand turn (38c & d)

In 1884, Cornelius Prather donated a piece of ground and built a one-room schoolhouse (37a). This was situated behind where the old Philo Post Office was located, on the west side of Highway 128 in the heart of Philo. It was approximately where the tasting room for the Baxter Winery now stands (37b). In 1891, for $1.00, Cornelius sold the land on which the Philo Methodist Church was built.

As the students increased over the years, and with the school being located very close to Cornelius's house, the noise was more than he could bear, so he donated another piece of ground farther to the southeast and a new school was constructed in 1895 (37c). The school, taught by just one teacher at a time who took care of all eight grades, was located on the exact spot where the P. G. & E. substation now sits (37d), just past the I. & E. Lath Mill on Philo School Road.

In the 1940s, the County of Mendocino consolidated all of the little schools, and the students were bussed to Boonville, resulting in the Indian Creek School being closed. It reopened in the early 1950s to cope with the influx of children that came with the logging boom. It stayed open for a few years until after the County Fair of 1956 when the children began attending classes in the unused fairground buildings. Over the next couple of years, the current elementary school opened, followed by the new high school in 1958.

37a. Philo School, 1880s

37b. Baxter Winery tasting room, 2013

37c. Indian Creek School, 1897

37d. PG&E substation, 2012

38. JOHNSON STORE / LEMONS' MARKET PHILO

Hwy 128: 23.00 mile marker in center of Philo—on the right

Around 1912 or so, George and Elizabeth Johnson★ constructed a large building in Philo and opened it as a mercantile store (38a). In 1914, the store burned to the ground and a larger store was constructed in its place, although this one was just one-story tall (38c). In both of these buildings, the local post office was situated on the far north side. Across to the far right side of the store and down some steps was a shed used to store feed and grain. Also just in front of the shed were two gas pumps. On the front of the store was a high porch in order to make it easier to load and unload wagons.

George and Elizabeth ran the store for many years, with Annie Reilly as postmistress from 1924 until 1950. The Johnsons sold it to the McKinney family who ran the store for a few years in the late 1940s and early 1950s, although the post office closed and a new one was opened across the street in 1951, with Marshall Winn as postmaster. (This one was to last for nearly fifty years, with Thelma Pinoli as postmistress for many of those years from 1972, before the current post office opened in October, 2001). The McKinneys eventually sold the business to Cecil Self, who added guns and ammunition to his inventory. In fact, he was showing a gun to a customer one day when it accidentally went off and scatter shot hit the ceiling—the remnants of the damage are still visible today if you look up, near to the entrance of the store.

After Self, the store changed hands a few more times—to Griffin, Valenti, and B & I— before Mr. Elmer Lemons and his wife June took over and opened on January 1st, 1973. Since then the younger generations of Lemons have continued to run this popular and successful business. They added a meat market and extended the back of the store out for more stock room. The building has been very well taken care of throughout the years and is a main hub of business in the Philo area (38b & 38d).

★ These Johnsons were the ancestors of the now-deceased Floyd Johnson and his son, Gary who, with mother Eva, wife Wanda, and the family owns the Johnson Ranch situated at the junction of Hwy 128 and Hwy 253, south of Boonville—the location of Burger Rock—see #8.

38a. G. W. Johnson Store, Philo, 1912

38b. Lemons' Market, Philo, 2012

38c. G. W. Johnson Store, Philo, 1921

38d. Lemons' Market, Philo, 2012

39. PRATHER HOUSE AND STORE / PHILO POTTERY INN

Hwy 128: 22.97 mile marker—on the left upon leaving Philo
(Currently the Philo Pottery Inn)

Sometime around 1899, Mr. John L. Prather, the son of Cornelius Prather, had a store (39a) that was located across a little gulch just north of what now is Philo (39b). He stocked most of the goods in the store in bulk form, such as coal oil in five-gallon cans, cheese in large wheels, and all sorts of dry goods and cooking utensils. He also had the first post office in Philo and was the postmaster simply because he had the post office in his store.

In 1912, G. W. Johnson built a big store just to the south of this location, on the east side of the road, that today is Lemons' Market (see #38). In about 1913 or so, John L. Prather closed his store and moved to Yorkville, and Johnson became the Philo postmaster, moving the post office to his store. It is not known when the John L. Prather store was actually torn down.

Prior to the establishment of the Prather Store, in 1881 Cornelius Prather, with the help of a Mr. Ward, built a lovely two-story house for the sum of $700 that sat back from the road, behind where the store was later developed (39c). It should be noted that Cornelius had a favorite cousin by the name of Philomena and it was after her that the town of Philo was named.

After more than 130 years the house has changed ownership several times. One of these started a pottery-making shop at this location and hence the name. In more recent times it has been a popular bed and breakfast, although currently it is a family home (39d).

39a. Prather Store, Philo / Highway 128, Early 1900s

39b. Philo / Highway 128, 2012

39c. Cornelius Prather Home, circa 1910

39d. The Philo Pottery Inn, 2012

HIGHWAY 128

40. DOC BROWN'S HOUSE
Hwy 128: 300' past the 22.50 mile marker—on the left

Doctor Brown's house, shown here in 1893 (40a), is located about one-half mile north of Philo and on the west side of the roadway. His full name was John Treble Brown, and his wife Elizabeth, a trained midwife, would ride on a pillion behind her husband on their horse whenever he went out on a call that needed a nurse. They had twelve children, four girls and eight boys. The sixth child, George Tansy Brown, married Florence Etta Beeson, the daughter of the famous Henry Beeson—one of the three gentlemen who first sighted the Valley in 1851 (see Discovery of Anderson Valley).

Doc Brown was also known to have a very quick temper, especially when a patient failed to follow his directions, although people would look forward to being invited to his house for a meal, as Elizabeth was known for her cooking skills and for being a very good hostess.

Doc died in 1903, one year after Elizabeth passed, and succeeding family generations lived in the house before, in 1963, the old house burned down. At that time the land was owned by Doc Brown's grandson, Mr. Arnold Brown, who built a new house on the same location. He was married to Louise Nicholes, the Valley's resident nurse.

Today, this is the home of Arnold's step granddaughter. She points out that the Concord grapevine in the first photograph was one of the first vines planted in the Valley in the 1860s and it is still there today—dominating the view of the house in the second photograph (40b).

40a. Doc Brown House, 1893

40b. Brown's House and grapevine, 2014

41. THE C.H. CLOW HOUSE
Hwy 128: 400' past the 22.16 mile marker—on the left

When Mr. Carl Henry Clow came to the Valley to settle, his first order of business was to construct a house for his family. This house was built around 1884 (41a) and was located about a half-mile north of the Doc Brown house, also on the west side of the road. Clow was known for his gardening expertise, and he planted a small orchard and farmed the land around his house. He became quite an authority on fruit trees and a 1922-1923 report from the Mendocino County Farm Bureau mentions that C. H. Clow expertly demonstrated in a public lesson how to go about pear-tree pruning.

The Clow family spread out throughout the Valley and engaged in several businesses, including a sawmill, a general store, and a working ranch. The short stretch of the highway leading uphill from north to south heading into Philo is still known as Clow Hill.

Sometime in the early 1900s the old Clow house burned down and a new house was constructed in the very same location. This too burned down in the mid-1930s and so another home was constructed in 1935 that became the home of Carl Henry's son, Carl Jr. and his wife Lois (Rawles). Carl and Lois passed it in to their daughter Jeanne Clow-Humphries, who in 1949 moved in to the house with her husband Jac and their daughter Joanne—the great granddaughter of the original C. H. Clow. Joanne remembers that the large old barn that still stands behind the house today was built in less than a week following a "community barn-raising" in which the community comes together to help with such a project.

Joanne later married Norman Charles, the son of the owner of the Charles' sawmill in Boonville. The eldest of their three daughters, Diana (C. H. Clow's great, great granddaughter), resides in the house today (41b), ensuring that for 130 years and counting that the Clow family and their descendants have lived in this location.

At one point our research into this property appeared to get very complicated. It was thought Carl Henry had a son Henry Carl, who in turn had a son, Carl Henry! We felt they knew they were going to confuse future amateur historians, and for a time they did. Fortunately Joanne Charles, Carl Henry's great granddaughter and a friend of the author Steve Sparks, straightened the history out and what you read above is the true version. The other version would seem to be the result of old-timers swapping tales at their daily coffee meetings and getting the Clow's sons and nephews mixed up. It made for a good laugh anyway!...

41a. Carl Henry Clow Place, 1884

41b. Diana Charles House, 2014

42. THE CLARENCE HULBERT HOUSE

Hwy 128: on the right, opposite Gowan's Oak Tree fruit stand
(approximately at the 20.75 mile marker)

Located across from the Gowan's Oak Tree fruit stand, a narrow lane runs off to the east, at the very end of which is the Clarence and Ruby Hulbert house. The property was originally owned by a Mr. Rhodes. Around 1900, it was bought by Arthur "Lolly" Gossman, who built a barn, and two years later, the house that still stands today (42a). Clarence purchased the place from Gossman in 1946 along with a considerable amount of land (120 acres) that had a large apple and prune orchard on it. Also included was a further 40 acres on the other side of the road, next to Hendy Woods.

Clarence and Ruby raised a family of six children in the house during some tough times, although the house did have their first flush toilet. The whole family worked in the orchard in order to produce crops of fruit each year, and they had a dripper and a dryer to prepare the French prunes before taking them to market. Clarence was also a very good sheep shearer and followed the sheep-shearing trail each spring and early summer.

Ruby was an expert pie maker and, with Clarence's help, would make around 250 apple pies each year to be sold at the Apple Fair in their stall, The Country Kitchen. Their small business was called "G & G Pies" which stood for "Grandpa and Grandma's Pies." Along with selling at the County Fair, they would take orders all year round and had 27 different varieties. Eventually, the County laws changed and required the family to have a commercial kitchen in which to make the pies—the house did not have that—so the business folded. However, daughter Pat, with help from friends, is keeping up the tradition of Ruby's Apple Pies, and continues to use her mother's recipes to make the pies that she still sells at the County Fair each year.

As time went by Clarence and Ruby both passed on and the children went out on their own, the ranch becoming unproductive and the cost of keeping it up prohibitive. It has been on the market for sale for some years with Pat still living in the main house (42b), and her nephew, Vincent (son of Pat's sister Marietta) and his family, and niece, Melanie (daughter of brother Harold) and her family, continuing to live on the ranch property at this time.

42a. Hulbert Ranch, circa Late 1930s (above)

42b. Hulbert Ranch House, 2011 (left)

43. SHIELDS SCHOOL / GOWAN PROPERTY
Hwy 128: on the right, at the 3rd turn past Gowan's Oak Tree.
(approx.20.30 mile marker)

This photo shows the Shields School in 1896 (43a). It is not known for certain when the school actually started, however it is believed to be around the mid- to late-1880s. This school remained in operation until in the late-1930s when Mendocino County consolidated all of the small schools and sent the pupils to the school in Navarro, six or so miles to the north. Later, following further consolidation and the closure of the school in Navarro, all the students would go to the schools in Boonville.

The school was located up on a rise on the east side of the road about ¼ mile south of what is now the junction of Hwy 128 and the Philo-Greenwood Road. It should be noted that back in the days of the school's operation this intersection was called Christine Junction.

A Mr. Devine bought the property from the school district and built the house that stands there today. Around 1960, Cecil Gowan purchased the house and land (43b), and it remains in the Gowan family today.

43b. Gowan property, 2013

43a. Shields School, 1896

Signal Ridge

(Left at 20.15 mile-marker on Hwy 128 on to Greenwood Rd.,
3½ miles to Signal Ridge. Turn left)

44. THE PRONSOLINO PLACE

Signal Ridge
Hwy 128: at the 20.15 mile marker turn left on to the Philo-Greenwood Road.
After 3½ miles turn left on to Signal Ridge (sign-posted).
The ranch is on both the left and right after ½ mile

In the late 1800s there were approximately 200 acres of wine grapes grown in the Greenwood Ridge area. In 1923, Giovanni (John) and Theresa Pronsolino bought the property on Signal Ridge and, with their three children, moved from San Francisco to the house on the ranch (44a). There were vineyards and apple orchards on the ranch as well as timber. Following prohibition, the grapes were sold to various wineries such as Sink in Cloverdale and Segghesio in Healdsberg.

The Greenwood / Signal ridge area became known as Vinegar Hill. Some people said this originated during prohibition days when folks would say they were going to the ridge for "vinegar" when they were really going for wine. However, long-time Valley resident Donald Pardini comments that all of his life he's heard "the reason it was called 'Vinegar Ridge' was because the wine was as sour as vinegar."

In 1940, the adjoining ranch of 80 acres was bought from the Pardini Family. It had a 10-acre vineyard of mostly Zinfandel grapes, and when he returned from World War II, one of John and Teresa's sons, Angelo Pronsolino, took over the management of the ranch.

In the early 1970s, Edmeades in Philo and Ridge in Los Altos Hills began purchasing the grapes and soon prize-winning wines were being produced and the vineyard became well known. Eventually, in 1976, the vineyard was sold to Dr. DuPratt, who was the father-in-law of Deron Edmeades. Today it is known as the DuPratt Vineyard but it has been sold and has now come full circle in that it is owned today by two of John and Teresa's grand-sons, Stephen and David Arieta, who purchased it in 2007.

Angelo Pronsolino became active in the logging and timber business and became an expert timber faller, eventually becoming the woods boss for the Philo Mill Company, but in later years he raised sheep and cared for the orchard. He married Eileen Brown, who was a daughter of the State Highway Superintendent, and they raised their family on the old ranch and still live on the property today (44b).

In June 2014, the last of the Pronsolino sheep were sold, signalling Angelo's retirement, and a poignant end of an era.

44a. The Pronsolino Ranch, 1930

44b. The Pronsolino Ranch, 2013

HIGHWAY 128

45. THE DAY RANCH

Hwy 128: 19.17 mile marker—on the right
(at Phillip's Hill Winery tasting room)

The first photograph (45a) shows the old house sometime around the late 1890s with the Day family in front. Records show that the house was built in 1857, making it the second oldest house in the entire Valley.★ It is unknown who built the house or who the original owners were, however a family by the name of Cowan owned the ranch prior to the Days owning it. Many years later, around the early 1980s, the place sold again to the Oswalds, who continue to be the owners today.

When the Days had the ranch, or possibly when the Cowans owned it, there was a large apple orchard planted on the many acres of flat ground. The Days constructed a large apple dryer about 150 yards out in front of the house. This dryer still stands in the same place, as does the house. When the Oswalds purchased the place it was a time when vine planting was really taking off in the Valley and so the apple trees were removed and grapes replaced them and remain there today.

The house is located about a mile north of the Philo-Greenwood Road and sits back some distance on the east side of the road (45b). The old house has been very well kept up and cared for over the years and to many old-timers is a well-known Valley landmark, while these days the old apple dryer at the side of the highway is the tasting room for Phillips Hill Winery.

★ The oldest, by a year or so, is Christine Clark's house—see #49.

45a. The Day Ranch, 1890s

45b. The Day Ranch, 2013

46. REILLY HEIGHTS

Hwy 128: 18.28 mile marker—on the right

The Gschwend family, who were among some of the Valley's earliest settlers in Anderson Valley in the early 1850s (see #49), had a daughter Christine who married Mr. James Reilly in 1877. James had their new house built in 1895-96, a beautiful home that became known as Reilly Heights. The construction of the house was near completion in this photo (46a). Unfortunately, their married life was poignantly cut short when James died at age 50. Christine went on to live to the grand old age of 102.

The lumber used to build the house was cut by the old Navarro mill, which was located at the mouth of the Navarro River. The lumber was hauled by horses and wagons up over the Navarro Ridge road to the town of Wendling (later know as Navarro) and finally on to the Reilly property. The house was built by a man named Henry Wightman, who also constructed two other landmarks in the Valley—the Ornbaun House on Highway 128 across from Fish Rock Road several miles south of Boonville, and the Titus House on Anderson Valley Way, neither of which can be seen from the public highway, unfortunately. The house was very well built, but despite this, during the 1906 earthquake the fireplace chimney was shaken down. The house has had some remodeling done but on the whole it remains the same, particularly from the outside—as can be seen.

For many years the house was lived in by Joel Reilly (James' son) and his wife, Winnie Atkinson. They had a son, Stanley Joel Reilly, who married local girl Donna Cox. Stanley and Donna Reilly (a current Valley resident) have three children, Jimmy, Kathleen, and Cindy, and seven grandchildren.

Joel and Winnie also had a daughter, Esther Reilly, who married Earl Clark, and they had a daughter, Christine Clark, James Reilly's great granddaughter. She presently owns the Reilly Heights with her son, Justin, whose family lives in the old house at this time. He is James Reilly's great, great grandson and, with his wife Christy, they have son Tristan, James' great, great, great grandson. Thus the old house has been the home of the descendants of the Reilly family for over 118 years and, given its very grand appearance, it is almost certainly the most photographed building in the Valley (46b).

46a. Reilly Heights, 1896

46b. Reilly Heights, 2013

47. COUNTS SCHOOL
Hwy 128: 18.07 mile marker—on the left

This school was established sometime in the early 1890s and was located on a sloping hillside over the banks of Mill Creek. It had always been a heavily timbered area but when the Stearns Mill began operating around 1900 they went even further and logged off most of the timber in the first decade or so of the century, leaving a barren landscape in which the school was situated (47a).

The school served as an educational center for the Christine area south of Wendling (Nevarro), but it was just one of the several one-room schools of that era. Around 1938-39, this school and other small schools were closed and the children were sent to the school in Navarro 4½ miles to the north. A few years later that school was closed and consolidated into the Anderson Valley School District and all of the pupils from that end of the Valley had to be transported to Boonville. Years later, the schoolhouse was purchased by the Reilly family and converted to a rental home (47b).

The bell, from the tower that was removed, remains on the property as a keepsake and reminder of the old days when this was a typical one-room schoolhouse of the late 19th century (47c).

47c. Counts School bell, 2013

47a. Counts School, 1913

47b. Reilly property, 2013

CLARK ROAD

(Left at 17.45 mile-marker on Hwy 128)

48. GUNTLY / DIGHTMAN / SCHENCK HOUSE
Clark Road—at the 17.45 mile marker turn left off Hwy 128
1st house on the left

The original house and property is believed to have been part of the Dightman Ranch, leased from the Guntly family from the 1920s to the 1940s. The first house (48a) burned down in 1926, and the initial section of the current house was built the following year, at the time that the Navarro mill was near the end of its operation. The Dightmans worked at the mill and at night used their wagon to haul lumber from the mill to build the new house. In earlier days, when the mill was in full swing and the railroads were used to transport the timber out of the woods, small cabins set on skids were moved on train flat cars and pulled out into the woods for the workers to stay in during the week. When the mill shut down these cabins were no longer used, so one of them was brought to this location (the train line was just across the road) and became a kitchen addition for the house.

In 1959, Bobby Glover, a Guntly descendant, used a tractor to pull the cabin (still mounted on its original redwood beam skids and containing a large wood stove) to its present location on the property. It was used as a summer kitchen, workshop, and storage, with an open-air woodshed added on. A new addition, with kitchen, bathroom, and laundry room, was then constructed onto the house.

In 1997, Marvin and Colleen Schenck bought the property and began significant remodeling of the house into a period Craftsman Style Bungalow (48b). Over time they also preserved the logging cabin. Prior to their remodeling, the place had fallen into a state of disrepair and was in dire need of renovation. The Schencks have done a splendid job, and the ramshackle old house is now a beautiful home that sits at the beginning of Clark Road.

(Marvin Schenck is a curator at the Grace Hudson Museum & Sun House in Ukiah and also a member of the Board of Directors for the Anderson Valley Museum and Historical Society.)

48a. Dightman Home, Circa 1925

48b. Schenck Home, 2014

49. THE JOHN GSCHWEND / CLARK HOUSE
Clark Road—2nd exit on the left, past Pinoli Ranch
(Photographed from ¼ mile to the east—Christine Landing / Handley Cellars)

In 1855, Mr. John Gschwend and his wife arrived and settled in the lower part of the Valley and built this house in 1856 with lumber from the newly constructed Gschwend sawmill (which was situated just west of what is the Mill Creek Bridge, near to Clark Road). It is shown here (49a) under construction and is the oldest house or building in Anderson Valley. They had a daughter named Christine who was the first Caucasian child to be born in Anderson Valley. This daughter married a Mr. James Reilly, whose family had come to the Valley from Ireland via Nova Scotia and Maine (see #46).

The house was located on a ranch later purchased in the early 1920s by a Doctor Thomas Clark and his wife, Bessie. They had a son named Earl Clark who married Esther Reilly, the daughter of Joel Reilly and wife Winnie, and granddaughter of James Reilly and Christine Gschwend.

Earl built a large apple dryer in order to dry and store the apples and have them shipped to market in the Bay Area. Later, he constructed large apple-packing shed in order to pack and ship fresh apples to market.

Earl and Esther lived most of their married life in this house and had a daughter, also named Christine, who today is living in this very house, and who is a valued Board member for the Anderson Valley Museum and Historical Society.

The second photograph (49b) is taken from virtually the same spot as the first—today this is in the Handley Cellars Winery parking lot on the other side of Hwy 128.

49a. John Gschwend House, 1856

49b. The Clark House, 2014

50. CHRISTINE LANDING AND KIRRY RANCH
Photographed from Clark Road—Gschwend / Clark House (#49)
(Hwy 128: 17.11 mile marker—on the right and left)

When the railroad was first constructed in this area, this was the end of the line (50a)—as seen in a photograph taken from near to the John Gschwend / Christine Clark house (see #49). However, later on, the railroad was continued on across this open area before turning and heading up Mill Creek for a few miles in order to haul logs from the Mill Creek canyon.

The railroad had previously been continued to this location from Wendling (Navarro), to bring lumber from the mill at Wendling. Down in the Soda Creek canyon, where the Wendling mill was situated (in current day Navarro), the sun shined for very few hours a day and the lumber would not dry. (Many Valley old-timers believe that to be the wettest and coldest place in the Valley—see #56.) By bringing the lumber inland to Christine Landing it could be stacked and dried.

The second photograph (50b), taken from the same spot as the first, shows that remarkably little has changed over the last century, apart from the Highway 128 replacing the railroad tracks, and of course a few vines here and there!

Oswald Kirry, his wife Josephine, and their family were one of the seven families originally from Switzerland who settled in the northwest end of the Valley in the winter of 1855. At least three of the families—those of Kirry, John Gschwend, and Andrew Guntly—had come from Madison County, Illinois. Oswald and Josephine raised their family, and Oswald became a wagon-maker and farmer.

For the time it was built, their ranch house was a very rare two-story structure (50c), known as the O.K. House, and it became the lodging and stage stop for the town. It can (just) be seen still standing in the far left of the circa 1920 photograph (50a) many years after the Kirry family had left the area They did so after 25 years in the Valley, following the 1879 divorce of Oswald and Josephine. Despite the split, both of them moved to Ferndale in Humboldt County. Two of their three sons, John Walter and Henry, stayed and ran the blacksmith shop in Comptche, later moving to Oregon. Josephine returned to the Valley and lived back in the very same area, near to the Guntly home (see #53). The old ranch house burned down in the late-1940s.

The Kirry Ranch, photographed around 1870 (50d), was in the Christine Landing area of the town called Christine. Today, the town would have encompassed what is Mill Creek, Handley Cellars Winery, Clark Road, the Pinoli Ranch, the lower Holmes Ranch Road and Guntly Road (Guntlyville as it was called), and Gschwend Road and its surrounding forested area known as Christine Woods.

50a. Christine Landing, circa 1920

50b. Christine Landing / Holmes Ranch (in background), 2012

50c. Kirry Home, 1870s

50d. Kirry Ranch, 1870s

51. M.I. DUTRO BLACKSMITH SHOP
Clark Road—beyond locked gate at vineyards

The first photo (51a), from about 1910, shows Mart Dutro and friends outside his blacksmith shop that was located slightly south of the Christine Store on the old highway, which is now at the end of Clark Road. Mart Dutro was a brother of Lou Dutro who was a timber faller in the days of the old handsaws. Mart was a very large and strong man as well as an expert blacksmith.

During those days, blacksmithing was a very important part of the timber industry because back then there were no electric or gas welders to construct metal parts together. The blacksmith would heat the metal parts to a certain temperature, add a flux material, and on an anvil would strike the parts with a large hammer and they would weld together. He would also heat and bend metal parts to form whatever they were to be used for.

There were several blacksmith shops throughout Anderson Valley at this time. This shop began operating around 1906. In fact, Dutro's son, "Kid" Dutro, had one in Boonville that is still there today, behind Rossi Hardware (#19). "Kid" had been a professional boxer, thus the name, "Kid" Dutro. He was also the bouncer at the Bucket of Blood Saloon (Boonville Lodge—#20). You didn't want to mess with "Kid."

At this time there was also a great need for someone to shoe horses—that was the main means of transportation in the area. Horses were not only used to ride or pull buggies but to pull large wagons loaded with bails of hops and sacks of dried apples, lumber, split railroad ties, and many other heavy loads. The old blacksmith shop was also a popular place for local ranchers and business people to meet and catch up on the local happenings and news of the area, but today the location is simply a part of a field of vines, although the old tree survives to this day (51b).

51a. Dutro's Blacksmith shop, circa 1910

51b. Vines and the old tree, 2013

52. THE CHRISTINE STORE
Clark Road—beyond locked gate at vineyards

The first photo (52a) taken sometime in the early 1920s, shows the old Christine Store with the owner, Cecil Brown, sitting in his truck. The small settlement of Christine was located about three miles south of Wendling, which today is known as Navarro. The little store stocked many items such as feed and grain, groceries, household items, and some hardware.

It is reasonably assumed that the area was named after Christine, who was a daughter of the early John Gschwend family and was the first Caucasian child born in Anderson Valley. The John Gschwend family (see #49), natives of Switzerland, arrived in the Valley's "Deep End" in 1855, along with six other Swiss families—Conrad, Gossman, Guntly (#53 and #54), Hauseman, Kirry (#50), and Schneider.

The old store has long since been torn down and all that is left of the location is a vacant piece of ground surrounded by grapevines. The road is long gone, replaced by Highway 128, as seen in the background (52b). This area of the town of Christine, on the edge of Christine Woods, was established around 1900 and is now almost completely covered by grapevines, apart from the wooded area through which Gschwend Road winds its way up the hill to the spot where most of the original Gschwend Ranch was located.

52a. Christine Store, 1920 (above)

52b. More vines and the new highway, 2013 (below)

Highway 128

53. ED GUNTLY RANCH (HANDLEY CELLARS)
Hwy 128: 17.26 mile marker—on the right

In the mid-1850s the Guntly family landed in this area of the Valley and Andrew Guntly camped under a large white oak tree upon arrival before building this ranch house for the family (53a). He was the father of Ed Guntly, who in 1911 raised the building up and expanded it, adding the ground floor and turning it into the large two-story house that stands in the spot today (53b).

The Guntlys homesteaded the ranch and later purchased land until it became a very large piece of property. After Andrew passed away the place was left to Ed, who began raising cattle on the ranch. One of the ranchers was Pat Hulbert's father, who would milk all of the dairy cows, morning and night, for rent, milk, and cream, plus 50 cents a day.

During the early boom days of the lumber mill and timber business they ran a slaughterhouse that provided beef to the mill camps in Wendling and Hop Flats. The one thing that makes this house stand out is not the size of it but the large water tank tower behind it.

The Guntly family sold the ranch in the mid-1950s to John Ornbaun, a realtor. Ornbaun passed away soon after and his widow sold the property to Ovid Holmes who went on to establish the Holmes Ranch Subdivision in 1972. This was when several miles of roadways were built on the ranch and the property was broken down into small parcels, 68 in total, and sold in parcels mainly 20 acres in size. The old house underwent some major reconstruction but the large water tank tower still stands out over the back of the house and is now part of the Handley Cellars winery and tasting room. The house is located on Highway 128, just north of Clark Road but on the east side of the highway up a slight rise.

53a. Ed Guntly House, 1880s

53b. Handley Cellars guest house, 2013

54. John Guntly Ranch / Rhys Winery

Hwy 128: 15.14 mile marker—on the right

In 1870, a European family by the name of Colson landed at this small opening about a mile south of Wendling. After staying there for a couple of years they decided it was too cold and damp for them so they sold the place to a Mr. John Guntly, whose family had arrived in this end of Anderson Valley in the mid-1850s. Between 1878 and 1880 John Guntly built the old house and barns that are shown in the first photograph (54a).

John Guntly was a descendant of the before-mentioned Andrew Guntly (see # 53), and he raised sheep on the ranch and made many improvements to it until he sold the place to a Mr. Ted Ingram and his wife Maud sometime around 1920. A few years later the Navarro Mill shut down for good and most of the people moved on to greener pastures. The Ingrams were unable to meet their mortgage on the place so in 1930 they sold part of the ranch, on the east side of the road, to a Mr. Frank Roux who ran sheep there.

Frank Roux ran his sheep on the ranch for a number of years until the late 1940s or early 1950s when he sold his part to a Mr. Nick Alexander, who converted the place into a horse ranch—Horse Haven Ranch. The old house was rented out to various people from time to time but was never very well taken care of. Finally it was unfit for rental and it sat vacant for several years.

Then, in 2008, the place was purchased by Rhys Vineyards, a large winery business from Santa Cruz, and they began to remodel the entire ranch (54b). In recent years the hillsides have been plowed up and grapes can now be spotted virtually everywhere the eye can see.

54a. John Guntley Ranch, circa 1885

54b. Rhys Winery, 2013

Wendling / Navarro

55. WENDLING SCHOOL / VACANT LOT

Wendling Street—at 14.50 mile marker, turn right off Hwy 128
Straight ahead

The very first school of the Laurel School District (see also Laurel School #59) was this one-room building called the Wendling School, built circa 1890s (55a). It was located in the space that is now vacant, between a house just to the north, the Namadao and Osana Pardini house, and what was once a machine shop (55b).

In the early 1900s a man named Joe Pedro built the large building with a big square false front on it—shown on the right in the second photograph. Joe was a good mechanic and blacksmith so he installed some heavy machinery inside the building in order to do repairs and welding and fabrication work for the mill. The building was a two-story structure and the upstairs was used many times as a dance hall. The old stairway still runs up the outside of the building leading to the dance hall.

After operating the machine shop, Joe opened up the REO automobile dealership and sold REO cars in the Valley. At that time there was no road from the coast except for a horse trail and buggy roadway, so the automobiles were brought to Albion by ship and offloaded onto railroad flat cars and then transported to Wendling by rail to a roadway.

Joe operated the business in the old machine shop for a number of years, then retired and sold out. It is unknown who purchased the place but it has changed hands several times since and has also stood vacant for quite a few years. In recent years the south side of the building became the home for a huge hive of honeybees. The undisturbed bees made their home in the walls and under the floor of the dance hall. Eventually the bees were retrieved as well as their honey, of which there were many pounds.

55a. Wendling School, circa 1899

55b. Osana Pardini House / Machine Shop, 2013

56. DOWNTOWN WENDLING / NAVARRO

Hwy 128: 14.30 mile marker—on the right

This first photo (56a), taken in 1906, shows the main downtown Navarro business area, or Wendling as it was called at the time. This is where the majority of the people stayed during the boom days of the sawmills and logging industry. These buildings were built around the early 1900s or so.

To the extreme far left in the photo is the corner of the Twin Hotels. Next, to the right, is the Toscano Hotel, owned and operated by the Pasero Family.

In the center of the photo is the third hotel called "The Hotel D'Italia." The Stearns Lumber Company constructed this building, intending to use it as a hospital for their workers, however it never was used for this purpose. Soon afterwards, Mr. Alciede Bacci, of Vinegar Hill, remodeled and converted it to a restaurant, bar, and hotel. In 1907, Joe and Sabatina (Mama) Pardini purchased it and it became known as "The Pardini Hotel." For the next 50 years, Mama and her sister Beppa served the finest Italian food that could be found in this part of the state. Later on, around 1962, there was some major remodeling done to the building and it became the Navarro Inn. Then, in 1974, it burned to the ground.

To the far right of the photo is the fourth hotel, the Ainslie Hotel, owned by Joe Ainslie. There is not much that could be discovered about this building and its occupants.

There has been much talk over the years of there being five hotels in the heart of Wendling / Navarro. Our research has found this to be unreliable information and it appears that there were just four. The fifth hotel was thought to be called the Navarro Hotel, located at a building a little to the south, but this turned out to be the Pasero family home and was never a hotel. Perhaps the confusion came from the fact that the Pasero family owned the Toscano Hotel. Or perhaps it was because in later years, as mentioned above, there was the Navarro Inn (not Navarro Hotel), but this was formerly the Pardini Hotel.

The little town of Wendling had its name changed to Navarro during the year 1913. The town originally took the name of a gentleman by the name of George X. Wendling. Mr. Wendling started up a shingle mill here on the banks of Soda Creek sometime around 1903. About 1906, or shortly thereafter, the Wendling shingle mill was purchased by a Mr. A.G. Stearns and the mill became known as Stearns' shingle mill. Stearns was a good businessman and expanded the shipping of shingles all over the country. Once a firm in San Francisco sent a very large order for shingles to Stearns in Wendling but the order was mistakenly sent to Wendling, Oregon, located about 50 miles northeast of Springfield, Oregon. This meant that Stearns missed out on a very large order that amounted to a lot of money lost. When he found out about the error he was heard to say, "We must change the name of Wendling." He contacted the United States Postmaster General in Washington D.C. and requested permission to use the postal stamp from Navarro-by-the-Sea, which was located at the mouth of the Navarro River and was by now an abandoned ghost town with its postal stamp no longer in use. As a result, in 1913, thanks to A. G. Stearns, the town of Wendling was officially renamed Navarro and remains as such today.

By the late 1930s, the demand for lumber slowed significantly and the Wendling / Navarro boom came to an end. All of those big old buildings have either burned down or have been torn down over time. Clearly today Navarro is a very different place to what it once was (56b).

56a. Wendling / Four Hotels, 1906

56b. Navarro, 2014

57. MILL BRICKHOUSE / NAVARRO STORE
Hwy 128: 14.20 mile marker—on the right

In the early years of Wendling, there was a company store run by the mill that served all of Wendling with food and supplies. During that time, a little to the south of the mill town, there was a brickhouse manufacturing the bricks needed for the mill's furnace—as shown in the first photograph (57a).

At this location, in 1908, a second store was built that was owned and operated by Jumbo and Betty Zannoni. Many years later it also housed the Navarro Post Office after the closure of the mill. The Zannoni's home can be seen in the background of the first photograph on the rise (and also in photo 60a), and the store was operated by the family for many, many years. It stood empty for several years until it was sold to Mr. Dave Evans in the early 2000s and he continues to run a remodeled version to this day (57b).

This store is located where it has always been, on the bank of Soda Creek just at the north entrance of Wendling Street, next to a beautiful grove of redwood trees, and it remains a gathering spot and the hub of activity in the "Deep End."

57a. The Mill Brickyard, Early 1900s

57b. Navarro Store, 2013

58. THE ICE HOUSE
Hwy 128: 14.12 mile marker—on the left

This building was originally constructed and used as a real estate sales location. After P. E. Lamar completed surveying the entire area of Wendlng in 1905, the ground was laid out in 50-foot-wide parcels and, in September of that year, W. T. Garrett and Company Real Estate began selling lots. (Today, due to this great land grab bargain, the lot lines surrounding Navarro remain mixed up beyond recognition.)

The team and wagon in front of the building in the photograph (58a) was the F. Estill meat wagon that delivered fresh meat to the stores, hotels, and ranchers. Later on, after the land office business failed, the property was purchased by Mr. Ernest Pardini, who bought it from a Mr. Bob Tyson, and it became the Pardini's home until several years later when they sold it and moved further south in the Valley. At some point, during the height of the mill town's success, this building became known as the Ice House as it is located in just about the coldest place in the whole Valley. Despite this, we are reliably informed that the building operated successfully as the town brothel!

The Ice House has since been sold a few times as well as rented out on a number of occasions. It is uncertain who owns the house today, however it has been well taken care of and remains a good-looking building. It is located just north of the Navarro store, on the west side of the highway (58b).

58a. The Ice House, circa 1905

58b. The Ice House, 2013

59. LAUREL SCHOOLHOUSE
Wendling Soda Creek Road: at the 13.97 mile marker
Turn right off Hwy 128
On the right

After leaving Wendling Street and "downtown" Navarro, almost one quarter-mile further north on Highway 128, there is a narrow paved road on the right side, heading east, named Wendling Soda Creek Road. About 300 yards up this street on the right side of the road there is a flat area where the old Laurel Schoolhouse sits. This is the second school located in Navarro (the first was the Wendling School #55), and it was built around 1908. This was a one-room school (59a) that had only one teacher who taught all eight grades. In the early days of the school, most of the pupils would walk to school from Mill Town and Wendling. Some of the pupils from the outlying area would ride horses to school. (It can also be seen clearly in photograph 60a taken in 1915.)

Over the period of a few years in the late 1930s and early 1940s all of the small outlying schools were gradually closed, this one being one of the last, when it finally shut down around 1942 and was consolidated into the Anderson Valley School District. As with all the other small schools, the pupils were then bussed to the school in Boonville. After its closure, this old building sat vacant for a number of years until folks from the Bay Area bought it, remodeled it, and made it into a house. From the outside it still looks like the old school house with the original school bell tower on the roof (59b).

59a. Laurel School, 1924

59b. Former Laurel School, 2013

60. THE WENDLING–NAVARRO MILL TOWN / THE HOLLOW

Hwy 128: 13.88 mile marker—on the right

The first photograph (60a), taken in 1915, shows an overlook of the mill town of Wendling. Some of the buildings previously mentioned can be seen here. The large building on the right side of the photo is the A. G. Stearns house, later the Zannoni House (mentioned in #57), and in the center is the Laurel Schoolhouse (see #59). In the left center is the Stearns' mill, and just to the right of it are the many small cabins used for the workers to stay in. Just below the mill can be seen the railroad tracks where they forked out. The large white building on the far lower left was the famous Ice House (see #58). Just to the right of the Ice House and across the railroad tracks can be seen a foot bridge crossing Soda Creek in order for the youngsters to get to the Laurel school. Also, the small building above the fork in the tracks was the jailhouse.

The second picture (60b) is a close-up of the mill town, also from 1915. The superintendent at the mill was James Reilly (see #46), while the foreman was John Reilly. The mill finally closed in 1929. Apart from the ones mentioned, virtually all of these buildings are gone. In fact, many of the shacks were moved to Caspar on the coast. The vegetation has grown back completely—as seen in the photograph below (60c) that shows the area at the side of Highway 128 just north of Navarro today.

60c. The Hollow, Navarro, 2012

60a. The Mill Town overview, 1915

60b. Wendling Mill Town, 1915

POST SCRIPT

Wes and the other historians know their Anderson Valley history and, together with Steve Sparks' further education in history (albeit the study of World War One), we feel a significant amount of experience was resourced when it came to working on this project.

However, the writing of history is a constantly evolving process, something that is re-visited, studied, and sometimes re-written. With this in mind, the authors are very willing to listen to and include any reliable but, by necessity, brief additions that could be added to these histories. They are also prepared to accept that there may be some corrections that folks wish to point out and if these have credibility then they can be made. As the book is printed individually on demand, or at most in small batches, any such alterations to the book can easily be done with each printing,

If such information needs to be passed on, the authors can be contacted through the Anderson Valley Historical Society (see below) or if you spot them around the Valley then stop them, offer to buy them a beer, and have a chat...

A.V. Historical Society: sheri@camprancheria.com
Cell phone: 707-357-1726

CPSIA information can be obtained
at www.ICGtesting.com
Printed in the USA
FSOW04n1655080417
32791FS